OTHER BOOKS BY BETTY DODSON, PH.D.

Sex for One (1987)
Liberating Masturbation (1974)

ORGASMS FOR TWO

The Joy of Partnersex

Betty Dodson, Ph.D.

HARMONY BOOKS

New York

Published by Harmony Books, New York, New York.
Member of the Crown Publishing Group,
a division of Random House, Inc.
www.randomhouse.com

HARMONY BOOKS is a registered trademark and the Harmony Books colophon is a trademark of Random House, Inc.

Printed in the United States of America

Design by Cassandra Pappas

Library of Congress Cataloging-in-Publication Data
Dodson, Betty.
    Orgasms for two : The joy of partnersex / Betty Dodson.—
1st ed.
    1. Sex instruction.   2. Orgasm.   3. Female orgasm.
I. Title.
    HQ31.D712   2002
    613.9'6—dc21   2002005935

ISBN 0-609-60985-8

10 9 8 7 6 5 4 3 2 1

FIRST EDITION

For all the gentle men who have enriched my life without coercion, abuse, or a drop of sexual violence. Like most women, I've had my periods of hating men. But once I understood the follies of my romantic love addiction, I was able to look back and appreciate my high school crushes, romantic lovers, two fiancés, a husband, and an abundance of postmarital sex partners both casual and profound.

Acknowledgments

WHEN MY EDITOR, Shaye Areheart, called and proposed I write the sequel to *Sex for One,* without hesitation I declined. No more frustrations working with a big corporation for me, thank you. She reminded me that a big publisher could also be a formidable partner. As we talked, I admitted that in spite of my reputation for being a career masturbator and a dyke, I'd been living with a young man for the past couple of years. And while I'd found our partnersex to be quite enjoyable, I still wasn't what I'd call a big fan of coupledom. Her enthusiasm and persistence finally seduced me into agreeing to write this book. My heartfelt thanks to her for making our collaboration so thoroughly enjoyable.

I want to thank my three brothers, Rowan, Bill, and Dick. Growing up with them allowed me to interact with the opposite sex as an equal. Otherwise I might have remained a closeted heterosexual.

My writing mentor, Grant Taylor, dropped out so I could do this book on my own and I thank him for that. Oh how I'd hated but then missed his incessant, literary nit-picking.

My two girlfriends who are both authors made some good suggestions. Marianna Beck of Libido.com thought I could let go of an entire chapter and I did. Maryann Macy covered the manuscript with a lot of helpful comments. My professional friends who are clinical psychologists and psychoanalysts working with clients asked me some hard questions about relationships that I couldn't really answer except to say my specialty is sexual skills. Still, their input was invaluable. My thanks go to Joanna Whitcup, Cathie Ragovin, Derek Polonsky, and Suzanne Iazensa.

I also want to thank my monthly women's group of Ph.D. therapists and sex educators who gave me feedback on the chapters I presented during our meetings. Although I nearly abandoned them during this project, my dear friends Mary Guarino and Joan McElroy cheered me on. The many phone conversations with Richard Lamparski kept my sense of humor intact.

Oh, I almost forgot. Without my new hip joints, I could never have experienced such fabulous partnersex again. Thanks to Dr. Robert Buly, my orthopedic surgeon, I'm still rocking and rolling.

Finally, I want to thank my roommate, Eric, who was my muse for this book. Besides putting in many hours reading and improving the manuscript, he was always there to calm me down or cheer me up with happy orgasms, lots of hugs, and sweet puppy kisses. When Eric's mother, Bonnie, read the book, I held my breath, expecting her to be shocked or upset by all the explicit sexual details about her son. Instead she said, "Everything you've written is true." Then she grinned and suggested I dedicate the book to her! It sounded just like a comment my own mother would have made. So I dedicate this book to my mother, Eric's mother, and to all mothers who are raising sweet, gentle sons.

Contents

Preface   *xi*

1   Liberating Partnersex   1
    The Myth of Foreplay

2   Heterosexuality Revisited   14
    Intergenerational Sex

3   Loving Love   25
    Romantic Love Junkies

4   The Bridal Shower   36
    We Haven't Come a Long Way, Baby

5   Loving Others   48
    Defusing the Power Struggle

6   Did You Come?   63
    The Mystery of the Female Orgasm

7   G–Spot or My–Spot   79
    Reaffirming the Clitoris

8   Masturbation for Couples   93
    Sexual Compatibility

9   Sex Toys   108
    For Couples Who Want to Have Fun

10 Orgasms for Two   126
    Intercourse with Clitoral Stimulation

11 Especially for Men   143
    World-Class Lovers

12 I'll Show You Mine   159
    Our Magnificent Sex Organs

13 Creative Partnersex   175
    Exploring New Sexual Skills

14 Rosebud   188
    Anal Eroticism for Heterosexuals

15 Sexual Seniors   202
    The Beat Goes On

16 Sex Coaching   215
    Teaching Sex in the New Millennium

    Afterword   231

Preface

WHEN THE TITLE of my book *Sex for One* was announced at my forty-fifth high school reunion in Wichita, Kansas, most people thought it was about sex for one at a time. In New York City, when I tell my friends the title of my next book is *Orgasms for Two*, they break out into a big grin and ask if I'm going to write *Orgasms for Three or More*. The answer is no, but now that I'm a senior citizen living with a young man, I am considering writing a book titled *Orgasms for Oldsters: Too Sexy for Their Rockers*.

After three decades of teaching women about orgasm through the practice of masturbation, I never envisioned writing a book about sex for couples. By the time I reached forty, I knew romantic love was a myth, relationships and marriages didn't last for me, and life wasn't fair. In spite of my vow to never fall in love or live with another man or woman again, my prized independence dissolved in 1999 when Eric Wilkinson moved in with me. After thirty years of living alone and enjoying the life of a bisexual bachelor, I was inspired by this young man to revisit heterosexuality. Only this time around I have the unique perspective of a financially and sexually empowered wise woman.

Sex for One was the result of the orgasmic sex I shared with my first postmarital lover, Grant Taylor. During the first year of our affair, in 1965, we discussed the important role that masturbation had played in our respective lives before we met. Once we included masturbation in our sexual repertoire, we also discovered that it enhanced partnersex. Since then we have continued our ongoing dialogue about the politics of masturbation. Today he is my trusted friend and brilliant Webmaster of www.bettydodson.com.

Orgasms for Two is a continuation of my erotic journey, sharing a positive message about how masturbation can liberate partnersex between gay male, lesbian, bisexual, and gender-blended couples. Because women are the ones who buy the most sex books, I offer a word of caution: This is not a book about how to get a man, how to keep him, or how to get rid of him or kill him after the relationship is over. I have no idea how to sustain hot monogamy or a passionate marriage. My personal record with both is dismal.

However, I do believe couples can be more realistic and down-to-earth by letting go of those sickly romantic expectations that drive us toward inevitable disappointments, insane jealousies, and murderous rages. After more than thirty years of teaching, I've got some practical ideas about how to improve sexual skills so men and women can share mutual orgasms. It is my firm belief that enjoying more sexual pleasure with ourselves as well as each other will make us all a little bit nicer, less violent, and more creative.

ORGASMS
FOR TWO

❧ 1 ❧

LIBERATING PARTNERSEX
The Myth of Foreplay

I T'S TOTALLY UNDERSTANDABLE why heterosexual men and women want to climax from penis/vagina sex—how convenient, how easy, and how wonderful to have partnersex be consistently and mutually orgasmic. However, if Romeo's firm penis moving sweetly inside Juliet's wet vagina provides orgasms for nearly every man and a mere handful of women, what are we going to do about the majority of women who cannot climax from vaginal penetration alone? We can broaden our definition of partnersex to include some form of direct stimulation of a woman's clitoris either manually or with a vibrator during heterosexual lovemaking.

Let's start with the concept of foreplay. Women's magazines as well as many sex books emphasize the importance of "foreplay" for couples. We are told that women want more of it and men don't do enough of it. It's been my observation that a little appetizer of kissing, breast fondling, and clitoral touching before the main course of penetration is seldom enough to satisfy the sexual appetite of most red-blooded women. Just as she is getting excited from some form of direct clitoral contact, he stops and penetrates her vagina. While he is enjoying his ideal erotic sensation with his

RIGHT ANGLE POSITION. *This is very comfortable for both the woman and man. She lies on her back with her knees bent while he is lying on his side with his body at a ninety-degree angle to hers. The leg positions will vary with couples. Either partner can provide direct manual clitoral stimulation during intercourse.*

penis moving inside her, she is now struggling to get a little indirect clitoral contact, which for most women can't compare to consistent clitoral stimulation all the way to orgasm.

Imagine a man being told he can rub his penis inside a woman's vagina as foreplay, but when it's time for his orgasm, she must be sitting on his face penetrating his mouth with her clitoris. This will give him a "mature oral orgasm." He must not reach down and touch his penis while she's fucking him in the mouth or she'll think her clitoris isn't big enough to provide his orgasm. To protect her female ego, he ends up faking orgasm, but he figures it's worth it to keep the peace. Later on he can masturbate in the bathroom, or if she's a sound sleeper, he can finish himself off in bed providing he can come while holding his breath and not moving so as not to wake her.

Instead of using the word "foreplay," we need to think of a new term to use, such as "sexplay." Most women desire clitoral pleasure in the beginning of, during, and sometimes even after partnersex, if she wants to come again.

As I enter the fourth decade of teaching women how to have orgasms, I've come to the conclusion that just as a man's penis gets consistent contact during penis/vagina sex, many women also want consistent clitoral contact throughout the entire act. Any man who is considerate will add direct clitoral stimulation with his fingers or a confident woman will stimulate her own clitoris with her hand, a little battery-operated vibrator, or an electric vibrator. Once the clitoris and the head of the penis are engaged, every thrust of his penis and contraction of her vaginal muscle becomes mutually pleasurable. They can share the ecstasy of orgasm during intercourse with few exceptions.

One of my basic principles for sharing mutual orgasms is: How we make love to ourselves is what we bring to partnersex. New designs for partnersex require a man who has learned ejaculatory control through the practice of masturbation and a woman who's learned her orgasmic response the same way. If he occasionally comes before she does or she feels like having another orgasm after he's been satisfied, there is nothing to prevent her from continuing. He can add sensuous touching or slow finger or dildo penetration while she continues clitoral contact with either her finger or a vibrator.

Another creative way for couples to share orgasms during partnersex is by taking turns. If she prefers oralsex for her orgasm, then after she has her climax they can go on to intercourse for his orgasm. If he prefers oralsex, too, they can flip a coin to see who goes first. Instead of seeing penis/vagina sex as the only thing on the menu, they can treat fucking as her appetizer and his main course. After he comes, she can have her orgasm with direct clitoral stimulation from a number of ways. For variety, lovers might choose to masturbate together and give themselves their own orgasm.

Over the years, my approach to teaching sex has been criticized by some and applauded by others. Some accuse me of being too focused on the body and orgasms. They believe love and relationships are far more important than cocks, clits, and sexual technique. Others are convinced that until we deal with the cultural, social, and economic inequalities in women's lives, sexual pleasure is a luxury most of us cannot afford. Some feminists believe we must end all forms of violence against women before we will feel safe enough to enjoy sexual pleasure. I disagree. One important avenue to improve women's lives and begin to end violence would be to defuse the war between the sexes.

In my opinion, experiencing consistent orgasms is essential in developing self-esteem and sustaining a loving relationship. During the twenty-five years I ran my masturbation workshops, the opening question, "How do you feel about your body and your orgasm?" made us realize how much confusion, pain, and unnecessary suffering sexual ignorance had caused us. We all agreed that both women and men would be happier and society less violent if everyone took a course in Orgasm 101.

When I was studying at the Art Students League in New York City, both teachers and students agreed that the creative process required complete freedom to explore our deepest feelings and convictions. Now, in my second career as a clinical sexologist, I feel the same way about human sexuality. Creative lovemaking also requires the complete freedom to explore our sexual bodies and our erotic minds. No religious organization or government agency has the right to tell us with whom, or under what circumstances, we can share our sexuality with other consenting adults. In any country that upholds the ideals of the democratic process, artistic and sexual freedoms go hand in hand.

Sex and art share other commonalities. Being a world-class lover or a first-rate artist requires skills that must be learned and practiced. Unfortunately, many people continue to believe that good sex comes naturally, as a result of an emotionally sound relationship. This idea has kept heterosexuality imprisoned for hundreds of years. Yet where do we go to learn the basics of how to erotically please ourselves, let alone another person? This is the challenge facing sex educators today, especially in America, where sex is a political battlefield as the boundaries between church and state continue to blur. The question is: Who owns our bodies, minds, and sexuality? Most would answer: Each individual does.

On the one hand, America flaunts sex in the media and entertainment fields, yet on the other, our Puritan underpinnings show through when we avoid the most fundamental, real-life aspects of sexual pleasure. Congress struggles with laws to restrict adult entertainment industries and ways to censor the Internet. Religious groups impose their beliefs on all students in public schools with government-funded, abstinence-only sex education that limits sexual expression to monogamous heterosexual marriage. Our teenagers are being told that birth control usually fails and abortion and homosexuality are morally wrong, and masturbation is never mentioned as a safe alternative to penis/vagina sex. Until

America accepts sexual diversity as the law of the land, to include gay men, lesbians, bisexuals, transsexuals, and intersexuals, we will remain in the dark ages of human sexual expression.

The religious and politically conservative people who are trying to control the dissemination of sex information claim it to be the domain of parents to teach their children. However, not all parents are in a position to teach sexual skills because many have never learned themselves. And by the time kids reach their teens, they don't want to discuss sex with their parents—it's too embarrassing. Those parents who enjoy their own sexuality will pass on positive nonverbal messages, and the clever ones will have a few good informational sex books on the family's bookshelves.

The next big chunk of sex information comes from children's peers, and it's often incorrect or distorted. I was six or seven years old the day my girlfriend Mimi told me that a baby would come out of a hole between my legs. I was horrified. No babies for me, thank you. Later, when I asked Mother if it was true, she said yes, but that having a baby was a beautiful thing. She explained that when I grew up and got married, my husband would put his penis inside my vagina and that's how a woman got pregnant and had a baby. She also said that having sex with a man I loved would be wonderful. From that day on I played with my nameless clitoris while dreaming of the moment my faceless husband would put his penis inside my vagina. What's wrong with this picture?

My first erotic drawing remains vivid in my memory. I was the best artist in school, so one afternoon at my friend Diane's house, several of my girlfriends asked me to draw a picture of sex. The image I created was a man on top of a woman. His arms were as stiff as the polelike penis disappearing between her thighs. I drew a small puddle of blood alongside her body to show she'd been a virgin. We were all heated up by my twelve-year-old rendition of sex—something we longed for and feared in equal measure. We talked about sex while ceremoniously sharing a few puffs on a cigarette that Diane had stolen from her mom's purse. Then I tore the drawing into little pieces and flushed them down the toilet.

Many people continue to believe that the man-on-top intercourse depicted in my first "dirty picture" is the preferred form of sexual expression. They say it's natural—God ordained it. But it is man, not God, who advocates the "missionary position," since it serves most men's need to control the action that leads to male ejaculation. In spite of the fact that this seldom provides orgasms for the majority of women, each new generation believes women should be able to climax from "normal" heterosexual intercourse.

I'll never forget the day, at age thirty-five, when I realized the awful truth about my own sexual ignorance. Despite all my years of childhood masturbation, teenage hand jobs, and seven years of sneaky marital masturbation, when it came to partnersex, it never dawned on me to make direct clitoral contact while having sexual intercourse. When I had an orgasm with myself I stimulated my clitoris, but when I had sex with a boyfriend, my clitoris became nonexistent. I was outraged to think it had taken so long to understand that my clitoris was my sex organ, and my vagina was the birth canal.

Now, after more than three decades of dispelling sexual myths, new ones have appeared. The Freudian vaginal orgasm goes by a new name: the G–spot orgasm. Today, sex stores all over the country sell G–spot dildos, along with books and videos that tell women how to ejaculate. Even though the vagina is not the correct term for a woman's sex organ, *The Vagina Monologues* made history worldwide. In our media-driven society it continues to be difficult to get an honest conversation going about the reality of female sexuality. However, in spite of all the current vaginal chic, I and many other knowledgeable people proudly wave the clitoral flag.

Women of all ages continue to show up in my office because they can't have an orgasm from vaginal penetration alone. Some have boyfriends who want them to learn how to ejaculate, but they can't find their G-spot. I'm beginning to sound like a broken record saying the same thing over and over: "It's great to have your individual preference for clitoral stimulation combined with vaginal penetration from a penis, dildo, or a finger happening all at once."

Whenever I carry on about the clitoris being our primary sex organ, someone always mentions a woman they know who has great climaxes from fucking only. Yes, I'm aware that a small percentage of women adore having orgasms with vaginal penetration and some enjoy spurting fluid during orgasm. However, I'm also aware that women have been conditioned to sexually please men for food, shelter, and protection ever since we lived in caves, so I take some of these reports with a grain of salt. How could I dare question a woman's personal testimony? Over half of the many women I've worked with admitted to faking orgasm to please their partners at one time or other. Some do it just to end partnersex.

Furthermore, we now have twelve-year-old girls giving blowjobs to boys before they reach high school *just to be popular,* and that's without any expectation of sexual reciprocation whatsoever. Instead of worrying about whether these children are having sex at too young an age, I worry more about the one-sided kind of sex that's taking place. Will these boys grow up expecting blowjobs without ever returning the favor? Will these young girls have enough self-esteem to feel they deserve sexual pleasure as adults? Or have they already been trained to sexually service a man in order to be loved and taken care of after marriage?

Men who are sexually skilled and love women have their own set of problems to deal with in partnersex. Besides making the date, deciding where to go, and picking up the tab, a man is also expected to initiate sex. He's usually in charge of getting her in the mood with kissing, sensual touching, and genital fondling. After figuring out a way to get both of them out of their clothes, he has to navigate his way among all the intricate folds of her labia to locate her clitoris and stimulate it with his tongue or fingers without any information about what she likes. Then he has to get and keep an erection, put on a condom, add lubrication, and find her vaginal opening. Once he penetrates he has to pay attention to the angle and the depth of his penis while holding back his orgasm.

In my youth, what made partnersex so wonderful was having passionate orgasms with a lover. What made it so difficult was my undying belief that romance, love, and sex would eventually come together and last for a lifetime. Meanwhile, society's financial and sexual double standard favors men, perpetuating an imbalance of power between the sexes. Due to religious beliefs, some women think their position in life is "naturally" subordinate to a man's, and they accept the status quo. But this inequality really pisses off the rest of us.

Allow me to paint a picture of heterosexuality with broad strokes. Women act as if they're dedicated to romance and love, but they're really more interested in financial security and marriage. Men go through the motions of romance and love, but they're really more interested in sex without commitment. Women use sex to get a man, but after marriage many lose interest because they are either nonorgasmic or it's too difficult to come during partnersex. Men promise to be good providers but they don't always succeed, or if they do, they become stingy misers after marriage. Some men never propose. Other men are already married, so she ends up as his mistress. Very few women are happy with a secondary role and scheme to change his mind.

There are many reasons why women don't like sex. First of all, young girls learn that partnersex is more about attracting a man than about pleasure and orgasm. After a woman falls in love, she is not guaranteed an orgasm, while her partner is assured of one during ejaculation. Women fear unwanted pregnancy and not all men are willing to be responsible. Some dispute their paternity. Extramarital sex is fairly common among men, and while more wives are beginning to have extramarital affairs, women are still the custodians of monogamy. Once jealousy enters the picture it begins to erode the joy in sex with doubts and suspicions. Very often, sex is a woman's only bargaining chip or weapon. The emotional baggage from childhood repression, fear of abandonment, and the ongoing power struggle drive the wedge of separation deeper. After a baby arrives, the woman usually has the lion's share of raising the child and partnersex often disappears altogether.

Allow me to paint another picture, this one of a world that includes sexual pleasure. Masturbation would be seen as a totally acceptable activity for children. Our middle schools would help girls and boys cope with the sexual urges brought on by puberty by encouraging self-sexuality. Along with the story of procreation, our teens would be taught the basic sexual skills necessary for sharing sexual pleasure. They would have access to birth control. Every young adult's first-time partnersex would leave a sweet memory upon which he or she could build subsequent pleasures.

Without adequate sex education or a history of successful masturbation, the first time a young woman has sex with her boyfriend she usually experiences pain, not pleasure. If birth control isn't used she faces weeks of fearing pregnancy. Sex is so disappointing that she focuses on the attention he pays her and the idea of being loved. On the other hand, if she has her first orgasm from his touching her clitoris, she either has to learn how to do it for herself or become dependent on him. In the latter case, she now views him as the source of her sexual pleasure.

Some people see no problem with orgasm dependency. Isn't that what love is all about? But what happens if her partner becomes abusive and she continues to "love" or need him? She is trapped in the cycle of love/hate while hoping he will change. Once financial dependency is combined with the responsibility of raising children, she continues to put up with his tirades or physical violence. She is a victim and he is an abuser, and together they are raising the next generation of women victims and abusive men. But abuse can go both ways. A man who is financially or sexually dependent on a woman can also be caught up in the cycle of verbal or physical abuse.

Men are also victims of female sexual repression. A nonmasturbating woman tells her partner she's never had an orgasm and he takes on the project of giving her one. He could spend years working on her lack of sexual response with countless hours of oral and manual sex, buying vibrators and trying everything under the sun to get her to come. But in spite of all his efforts, she is unable to climax. Some women get a lot of mileage from all this attention. Other women feel so bad that they can't come after everything their partner has done that they end up faking orgasm and getting trapped in a pattern that's difficult to break.

Some rape or incest survivors are unable or unwilling to move on, to sexually heal themselves with therapy and masturbation. And their partners suffer for their early misfortune. The healing process for sexual abuse takes time and is often complex, but can be done. A friend of mine was raped at knifepoint but was determined to fight back by regaining her enjoyment of orgasms. She felt that doing otherwise would mean the rapist had won, had destroyed her sexuality. For a woman who has never experienced any sexual pleasure, not even with masturbation, the road to recovery can be difficult indeed.

We seldom hear how male masturbation affects partnersex. Being a quick ejaculator is often the result of doing fast masturbation to avoid getting caught or not masturbating at all. Once these men penetrate a vagina, they last only a few moments before shooting their load. At the other end of the scale, a young man I know grew up humping a rough shag carpet in his bedroom. Now in his late twenties, he can't get enough stimulation from a vagina to climax. On the one hand that means he can last for some time, which pleases some women. However, when he wants to come, he needs a lot of stimulation, and hard, fast friction inside a vagina can be painful to a woman. He finally discovered that when his girlfriend used a vibrator on her clitoris while they were having intercourse, the added stimulation also helped him to orgasm more easily.

Until we acknowledge and accept masturbation as the most basic form of sexual expression we will continue to be a nation of fast-ejaculating men and nonorgasmic women. Through the consistent practice of masturbation, girls can become orgasmic women who are rarely victims because they have self-esteem and can speak their minds. They look forward to enjoying partnersex. Boys who have trained themselves to control ejaculation will become men with sexual self-assurance who are less prone to violence. Masturbation allows both boys and girls to develop their sexual feelings, make better social adjustments, and, by lessening sexual frustration, improve the quality of their lives. Sexual repression—not the expression of human sexuality—is society's enemy.

As we begin to unravel the economic and sexual inequalities that maintain the sexual double standard and the power struggle between the sexes, we can be more honest about what turns us on instead of using sex to manipulate the partner who holds the purse strings. Instead of having every sexual encounter a test of masculinity or femininity, we can relax and enjoy sex for the simple pleasure of it. Rather than seeing partnersex as a serious matter that defines the depth of our commitment and love, we can see it as a delightful form of adult play that remains in the present moment without making demands on the future.

Change is a slow process, but I do see some improvement. A few more sexually informed young couples are exploring what turns them on through an open dialogue about sexuality. Married couples have said that watching each other masturbate has spiced up a lagging sex life. Mothers have talked with me about not interfering with their children's natural sexual exploration with masturbation. More women are dispelling myths about romance, and they are no longer confusing good sex with falling in love. Survivors of sexual abuse are healing themselves by learning how to experience pleasure with the consistent practice of self-sexuality. Couples who choose to be monogamous are agreeing to a single standard. A brave few are even questioning the ideal of monogamy by confronting jealousy and allowing more sexual freedom in their partnership.

These changes are the result of couples' realizing that there is no one "right" way to have partnersex. Every sexual dance has a different rhythm. When we add the mental stimulation of sexual fantasy, the range of differences becomes infinite. There are a multitude of variations on how a clitoris or penis can be stimulated during intercourse, so there is no reason to limit sex to the procreative model. Instead, we can include all the wonderful things we can share with our lovers by touching, kissing, and licking each other's faces, bodies, and genitals. No one gets enough affectionate hugging and kissing.

Sexual fulfillment is our birthright and belongs to individuals and couples of every sexual orientation, both young and old. Experiencing more sexual pleasure just might end some of the wars being waged behind the closed doors of America's nuclear families and domestic partnerships. With more physical affection and closeness, couples can begin to negotiate boundaries, express their feelings, request changes, and express their gratitude for what is working in the partnership. Sharing mutual orgasms is essential in liberating and healing partnersex of all persuasions by bringing couples closer together.

❦ 2 ❧

HETEROSEXUALITY REVISITED

Intergenerational Sex

E VERYONE HAS A RIGHT to keep his or her sex life private. The reason I'm willing to go public with mine is because it's been proven to me time and again that the most effective way to teach something as subjective as sexual pleasure is by using the power of example. Since the seventies, I have shared my challenges and successes in the process of exploring sexual pleasure. What is happening to me in terms of my sexuality is not an isolated incident taking place in a vacuum. The chances are good that many other people are dealing with similar issues.

Although the idea of pleasure might be frivolous in a world that appears to be on the brink of horrible disasters, I believe one of our best hopes for survival depends upon embracing and celebrating human sexuality as a healing force.

As a seeker of sexual pleasure, I have tried many different

lifestyles. In my twenties, it was romantic love with hot sex along with the inevitable pain and suffering of breaking up. The first part of my thirties was love and marriage with minimal sex while I enjoyed the illusion of security. When I got divorced, I was back to romantic love, until my lover and I discovered threesomes and group sex. By my forties, lighthearted sex with both women and men greatly expanded my exploration of sexual pleasure. After AIDS shut down casual sex, the women's lesbian and bisexual SM community captured my imagination and spiced up my post-menopausal fifties.

Following an extended hiatus from heterosexuality, I succumbed in my sixties to the desire for a little old-fashioned fucking with men again. Straight sex even seemed a bit kinky. Over the next few years, I discovered that there were very few age-appropriate men with the sexual skills or stamina to match mine. Older men weren't turning me on, but it was no big deal. My women friends were emotionally satisfying, my private practice was doing well, and producing videos had my creative juices flowing. I was content to let heterosexual fucking remain a fantasy for my delightful sessions of self-loving.

For several years I'd been masturbating with a vibrator on my clit, doing slow penetration with a sapphire blue dildo while fantasizing about sex with a handsome young man. Maybe I mentally pulled him in from the electronic highway. While I was going over my e-mail one day, a question caught my eye. What exactly did I mean when I used the term "suction fuck"? In my book I contrasted it with "friction fuck," which seemed self-explanatory, but it wasn't enough detail for a man seeking explicit sex information—something that rarely happened. Men usually acted as if they knew everything about sex.

My response explained that "suction fuck" was when a woman consciously used her pelvic floor muscles during partnersex. As the man pulls out, she squeezes her vaginal muscle on his penis and releases it as he goes back in. Using slow fucking motions allowed both partners to feel more genital sensations rather than the usual fast friction fucking we so often see in film and porn. It was okay to move a little faster just before orgasm, but not to go at it like rabbits the entire time.

Eric Wilkinson was about to graduate from college with a degree in English. He was also sexually precocious. He told me he'd studied all the important sex books and he thought the ones by women made the most sense. *Sex for One* was one of his favorites, so right away I knew he was smart. Over the next few months his e-mails were my favorite masturbation material. His descriptions of how he'd designed different sex scenes with his girlfriends showed signs of the artist—someone who paid attention to the smallest details.

One night after reading one of his e-mails and having a fabulous orgasm, I invited him to come see me—fully aware that I might be risking the loss of my fantasy lover after we met. I offered to show him a few advanced sex techniques if he ever got to New York. I felt it wasn't likely to happen because he lived in Virginia, but it was fun to imagine.

He answered my e-mail promptly, saying my invitation was a great honor. He'd always dreamed of having a woman "sex master" teach him advanced sexual techniques instead of struggling with the usual trial and error. We made a date to meet during the Christmas holidays, which were several months away. To cover my back, I requested that we have lunch first and talk. If we both felt positive about his being a student and I his mentor, we could continue; if not, we could part with no hard feelings. He agreed.

On the designated weekend, he was to call Friday night when he got to the house of a friend who lived in Queens. When I didn't hear from him, a dark cloud of paranoia settled over me. Had some twisted person seduced me with a young virile man's sexual fantasies? The media had been filled with sensational stories about cyberspace creeps who made dates with gullible women, some ending in disaster.

That night when I went to bed, I was angry with myself for offering to have sex with a total stranger. I was insecure about my aging body whenever I had sex with a man, especially for the first time, but I never felt judged by other women. If it weren't for the exhilarating rush of leaping into the erotic unknown, I would never have considered dipping back into heterosexual adventuring after menopause, especially with a much younger man.

I was shocked the next day when the doorman announced Eric's arrival on the intercom. Waiting for him to come up in the elevator, my heart pounded with fear and excitement as adrenaline pumped through my veins. As he entered the foyer, I caught my breath: six feet tall, dressed all in black, in a suit with a vest and a crimson tie under a full-length topcoat. His short dark hair set off a handsome face that had a distinctive sharp nose, piercing deep-set eyes, and a full sensuous mouth framed by a pencil-thin mustache with a devil's goatee. He could have stepped out of the pages of Anne Rice's vampire books: a mysterious man, dark and sensual, yet just under the surface I saw the boy who was fresh, bright, and a bit self-conscious.

He apologized for not calling. After some small talk he began describing how during his years of frequent and extended sessions of masturbation he'd been practicing what he called "come control." He confessed that when he had sex with a partner, he usually ejaculated during the woman's final ascent to orgasm, but he always finished her off with oralsex. After his first orgasm, he could get another hardon and then last longer.

A surge of raw desire flared within me as I listened to this beautiful man speaking so openly about his sexuality. I definitely wanted to fuck him. Making a wise decision, I asked how he felt about forgetting the roles of teacher and student and just enjoying each other. He grinned, saying it was fine with him. Putting us on a level playing field allowed me to move out of the familiar role of teacher with my vulnerability safely guarded in an ironclad Ph.D.

As I had done in hundreds of workshops, we undressed in the foyer and hung up our clothes. Then we entered my living room, which for three decades has been devoted to the pursuit of pleasure. We sat opposite each other on the soft zebra blanket spread out on the carpet in the warm room and talked about many things. He showed me his system of martial arts breathing and I shared mine from yoga. We talked about playing safe and I showed him the bowl of condoms I kept on the shelf with a bottle of water-based lubrication and massage oil. Lying just under the table, next to a chair that I used for my private sessions, was an electric vibrator that was always plugged in. My favorite dildos were displayed on another shelf.

When he asked if he could "taste me," I smiled and nodded, knowing he intended to begin with direct clitoral contact—smart man. As I lay back on the soft blanket, I relaxed into some amazing vulva worshiping. It was delicate and sweet, no automatic routine, only tenderness and creativity. His unspoken message was: "I'm thrilled to do this and I'll be here as long as you want." His attitude was so positive that I sank into all the delicious sensations. Unless a person was HIV positive, I didn't see kissing or oralsex as a high-risk activity.

As his soft, full lips embraced my cunt, his mouth filled with thick saliva, keeping everything wet. Flexing his tongue, he teased and circled my clitoris, varying the rhythm and keeping the pressure easy and light. Then, flattening his tongue, he covered a larger area, followed by an erect tongue probing my vaginal opening. The whole time his fingertips and palms drew circles on my belly and breasts. His hands were beautiful—large with long slender fingers—and he used counterpoint rhythms—fast tongue, slow hand; firm massage and feather lips. With each breath I took, trust was building steadily as my body climbed the sexual arousal ladder.

Lying on his stomach between my legs, his graceful fingers moved in between my vaginal lips. A finger glided into my vagina, another gently massaged my anus. His tongue stayed with my clitoris as both fingers began moving in and out of both openings. It was a sensation so erotic I groaned aloud with shivers of pleasure. Later, when I complimented him on his rhythm and manual skills, he said he'd studied the piano for eight years.

Next he asked me to turn over. He was so bold, yet so sweet, that I found myself sinking deeper and deeper into the unfamiliar state of sexual surrender. When it came to partnersex, I was always the one who ran the show—in control. He asked me to put both of my legs together to "preserve the line of my body." Beginning at my knees, he oiled my back, legs, and behind. Then he slowly moved his hard velvet cock upward in between my thighs and ass cheeks, and then back down again. Over and over, he moved up and down with one long smooth motion, never pausing a moment. The exquisite sensation made every nerve ending come alive.

After what seemed like an eternity of pleasure, I was overwhelmed with the desire to have him inside me, and I heard my voice pleading softly, "Eric, please fuck me. Please." I heard him tear open a condom. A moment later, when the head of his cock pressed into my vagina, I tilted my pelvis up slightly and he slipped in effortlessly. As he moved slowly in and out, I squeezed and released my vaginal muscles, savoring the exquisite sensations of our suction fuck that undulated on and on. What a luxury.

My level of excitement peaked. As I rose up on my hands and knees, he moved with me, and without missing a beat, he continued his slow, smooth movements as we fucked doggie style. Taking hold of my vibrator lying nearby, I threw the switch and held it near my clit. Consumed by lust, I twisted and turned—impaling myself on his hardon. He held firm so I could move with abandon. Strange sounds like those of an animal in heat came from my mouth as I began moving more urgently. While in the throes of this ecstatic state, I heard his sweet voice say, "That's it, angel. Enjoy yourself."

My orgasm took me with such force that my body shook and quaked until I finally fell into a trembling heap, crying hot tears of relief while laughing with joy. He finally let go and had his orgasm while I was still shuddering with aftershocks of pleasure. I rolled over and both in a state of awe, we wrapped our bodies around each other, savoring the afterglow of sensual wonder.

This was all so unexpected. How many years had it been since I'd had such a powerful orgasm with a man? For a moment, I silently wondered if an alien had been sent to prepare me for the erotic evolution of the new millennium.

The next morning and again that night, we continued our sexual dance. At one point I insisted he state his pleasure—a first for him. The young women he'd had sex with expected to get done without doing much of anything in return. Now that it was his turn, he wanted to experience both oralsex and anal penetration combined for the first time. After all his generosity, I was delighted to please him. Using both my hands and mouth, I gave him a first-rate blowjob, including several moments of deep throat. His lovely firm cock strained against the pleasure but held on inches from release.

Then he got on his hands and knees, and as he leaned forward in the knee-chest position, I oiled his sweet buttyhole with tender loving care. While I was moving first my finger and then a dildo slowly in and out of his bottom, his hand was making short delicate strokes on the head of his dick. He bellowed like a dragon as he came full force. Afterward, he said for years he'd dreamed of doing these things and they turned out to be better than he'd ever imagined. I laughed and said, "Me, too."

During our separation we talked on the phone. Part of me was convinced that I was losing it. Another part was just soaking up the pleasure. My guarded independence was gradually dissolving as I tumbled head over heels back into heterosexuality. All of this was taking place when most women my age are showing off photos of their newly born grandchildren.

Eric returned for another week and the sex we shared was even better. Then he asked if he could return in the spring and stay for a month. He kept talking about how he wanted to be my apprentice and carry on my work. Against my better judgment I kept saying yes to him.

At first I saw Eric's time with me as limited to a short period of sexual fun, but within six months he had replaced my assistant and was running my business full-time. We were having partnersex nearly every day. What a delight to be fucking whenever we felt

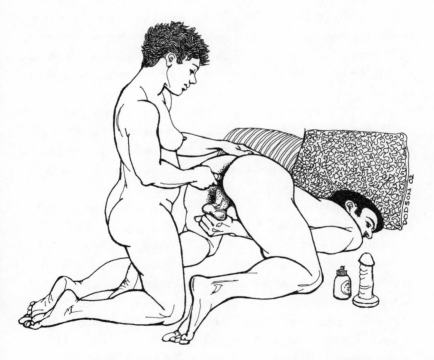

ANAL PENETRATION. *Here, a woman doing anal penetration on her partner while he stimulates his penis. All forms of anal penetration must be done slowly, with an abundance of lubrication and gentleness. The receiving partner needs to be sexually aroused before penetration takes place. To facilitate relaxation, he or she also needs to know how to squeeze and release the pelvic floor muscles.*

like it without any concern for birth control or condoms. Our decision not to use a condom was based on our sexual histories and the fact that we'd both tested negative. He'd had sex with a handful of young women who were virgins, except for one or two who were sexually experienced, and he had always worn a condom with them. I'd had penetration sex with very few men in the past five years and they also had used condoms. Since menopause at fifty, I'd had most of my partnersex with women using dildos, vibrators, and fingers—just about as safe as one could get.

I always enjoyed watching Eric move around the apartment naked—a living work of art with his broad shoulders narrowing down to a firm, tight ass with strong, muscular legs and a perfectly sized penis. His playfulness continued and with his perpetual hardon, he was available for any kind of sex. I'd found the perfect boy toy.

Meanwhile, I kept expecting him to get a roommate and move into his own place so I could reclaim my apartment. I knew it was a disaster for two people to live, work, and have sex together under the same roof—a dynamic I counseled couples to avoid. On top of that, I'd promised myself to never have another roommate or to ever live with a lover again—been there, done that. It was painfully clear that I was breaking all my own rules.

At the end of our first year together, I finally stopped trying to get rid of him and worrying that he was young enough to be my son. Instead, I embraced the joy he brought into my life. I decided he was a divine gift from the universe, my reward for three decades of promoting masturbation and teaching thousands of women how to have orgasms. I began to graciously accept his bright shining presence in my life.

While I was struggling with the idea of having a sexual relationship with a man in his twenties, the world watched President Clinton's popularity ratings climb as the media had a feeding frenzy detailing his affair with a twenty-one-year-old woman. My own maternal grandfather married a girl younger than his oldest daughter. Many famous men have had young wives, from Picasso to Charlie Chaplin to Justice Hugo Black. The combination of older men with younger women has been an acceptable part of history since the beginning of time. Society accepts and even admires men who do this, but if an older woman claims the same rights, it threatens our authoritarian society, which wants to maintain the sexual double standard. I simply decided to enjoy the same privilege that men have always taken for granted.

In many ways our mentor/student relationship makes sense historically. Tribal cultures had older aunts and uncles teaching sex to the young people. In the Tantra, or Buddhist, tradition, older women were the teachers. My Native American ancestors had a tribal Fire Woman, a wise elder who taught sex to the young braves. When people worshiped a female deity and human sexuality was revered, the goddess's consorts were virile young men whose sole purpose was to provide sexual pleasure to the Divine Orgasmic Mother of us all. We know there have been periods in history when sexuality was seen as a spiritual practice, or at least a natural and healthy part of being human. Besides, there isn't a single discipline on the planet that doesn't value mentoring.

Since I've been living with Eric, I've gotten a lot of kidding from friends who take an excessive amount of pleasure in reminding me of all the years I bad-mouthed couples who were joined at the hip. I often referred to them as living in "pair-bondage" and would detail the pitfalls of these codependent relationships to anyone who would listen. Needless to say, I was brutal when it came to criticizing romantic love, which I equated with stepping into dog shit—it's purely accidental and it takes forever to get rid of the smell. I know because I've had a lot of experience falling in romantic love with men who could never meet my expectations.

After living as a committed single for nearly two decades, retracing my steps through heterosexuality was unexpected, troublesome, demanding, and a delightful expedition. Make no mistake: This time around I'm under no romantic illusions about our intergenerational erotic friendship. Given the best of circumstances, the idea of two people living together while expecting great sex to be part of the picture indefinitely is highly improbable or akin to a miracle. It amazes me why more people don't question the sanity of trying to make the world come in twos, like the animals boarding Noah's ark. Okay, okay! All of this pairing off business is probably sexually driven. When partnersex is good, I'll be the first to admit, it can be quite extraordinary. Maybe that's the reason we're willing to pair off—we get hooked after a few ripsnorting orgasms with a person and say "I do" or ask them to move in with us.

Now, several years later, every word I said about the impossibility of two people living, working, and having sex together under the same roof is absolutely true. However, it led to writing this book, so maybe Eric was meant to be my muse. There have, of course, been trade-offs and sacrifices as well as joys and comforts in having a significant other in my life. When I weigh the pluses and minuses, we remain well on the plus side of pleasure. Nothing is etched in stone and we both remind each other to stay in the present and not to project into the future.

He has heard all the accusations about having a sugar mama, being a star fuck, a gold digger, and a mama's boy. I've been told I'm robbing the cradle, spoiling him, and because of me he'll never grow up. His friends think I'm taking advantage of him and my friends think he's taking advantage of me. While all of this may be true, it's precisely our age difference that allows us to be so compatible, enjoy great sex, and have so much fun together. We are both equally dedicated to exploring and refining the art of partnersex. I adore having him as my apprentice, my assistant, and my consort. Before jumping to any of those seductive romantic conclusions, let me assure everyone: We are not monogamous and I don't expect our erotic love to last "forever." It will last for as long as it's good.

❧ 3 ❧

LOVING LOVE

Romantic Love Junkies

THOSE SEEMINGLY HARMLESS FAIRY TALES my mother used to read at bedtime were just the tip of the iceberg of my female conditioning. Similar to each successive generation of little girls, I grew up dreaming of being kissed awake and saved from a life of drudgery by my very own prince. Sleeping Beauty and Cinderella were my first role models long before Sheena, Queen of the Jungle or Wonder Woman ever appeared in comic books. As a child I was surrounded by sentimental symbols of heterosexual romance: lacy valentines with plump red vulva hearts pierced by Cupid's phallic arrows. My mind was filled with love stories that promoted imaginings about love and marriage that had very little to do with reality. Living my life based on a romantic myth is what I call loving love.

Young girls who have been taught that one special man will bring them love, happiness, and security often have a serious handicap. Many women end up desperately struggling to become fully grown adults who are capable of intelligently dealing with life on its own terms. We believe we need a man to protect and support us. Loving love blinds us to the cold hard fact that getting married doesn't mean our futures are secure. More than half of all wives will get divorced and end up supporting their children and themselves. A wise woman once said that to the degree a woman allows herself to be ruled by the emotions of love, she has surrendered her status as an adult.

Research has shown that falling in love produces chemical changes in the brain, causing feelings of euphoria that enhance sex and even life itself. But what is this thing called love? If we describe love as a strong sexual attraction, then it could be seen as a delightful drug that keeps couples high until reality enters the picture. Knowing this, we might want to avoid making major decisions, like getting married or moving in with someone, when we're high on love. Then again, a strong sexual attraction is one of the best barometers to forecast a successful partnership. This business of love and sex poses quite a dilemma.

Given my own history, along with years of listening to other people's problems, I would never underestimate the importance of sexual compatibility or the power of having consistent orgasms with one's partner, especially in the beginning of a relationship. When I got married, I actually made a decision to be "in love" even though our sex was problematic. I would never have admitted this at the time, but I was bored with dating and desperately wanted some kind of financial security. We played the roles of the adoring romantic couple, using every age-old symbol of romance: sweet love notes, the single red rose, displays of affection, and constant verbal statements of "I love you."

The desperate search to find my other half was the most compulsive/obsessive aspect of being an all-American girl. This desire to be paired off with all the gooey romantic trappings of a bad romance novel was similar to belonging to a religious cult. After I got married and found myself living with a man who didn't care that much about sex, I was devastated and blamed myself. I'll never forget feeling I was a failure as a woman. Then I sank into resignation as I sublimated my sex drive into art by painting day and night. Even after seven years of surrendering to the daily routine of reality, I remained a romantic love junkie who had married the wrong man.

Romance novels and fashion magazines are to women what pornography is to men. Since fewer women seek money, power, fame, or fortune as compared to men, we want a love story full of excitement and romantic adventures. As a married woman, my porn was *Vogue* magazine. I imagined myself in various fabulous outfits about to go on an exciting trip or a cruise. Of course, looking at photos of beautiful fashion models also depressed me, because I could never measure up. Then I would succumb to my dirty habit of masturbation and vow each time to stop. This was during the early sixties, when pubescent girls with hormones surging though their bodies screamed and fainted at Beatles concerts while I scoffed at the absurdity of such foolishness.

Long forgotten were the childhood nights I'd laid in bed dreaming of my own noble prince as I secretly pressed my hand between my legs. As a preteen, instead of swooning to Frank Sinatra, I was masturbating to the fantasy of my wedding night: While my husband waited for me in bed, I went into the bathroom to prepare for our first night of passionate sex. I imagined myself as a beautiful woman, with thick, lush hair. My breasts were full and round. My teeth were movie-star white and even. As I mentally applied makeup to my perfectly clear skin, my breath came in hot little gasps. My pulse raced faster as I went over the details of the lace dressing gown that showed off my gorgeous body and boobs. Entering the bridal suite, I dropped the gown to the floor and that's when I came—each and every time.

I was my own sex subject and object, dreaming about being a

beautiful woman desired by a faceless man. Why is it that so few
women look at pictures of handsome men and imagine which one
they will choose? Maybe beautiful women can afford to do that, but
average-looking women can only dream of being chosen by Mr.
Right. More often than not we end up with Mr. Wrong. It's a spin-
off from the sexual and economic double standard where men get
to choose and do the asking because they usually make more
money and therefore have more power.

Traditional sex roles were barely affected by the women's movement because most feminists didn't want to abandon the universal
dream of finding a prince or princess to love, marry, and live with
happily ever after. Loving love masks women's ignorance and stifles
the ability to learn how to communicate, negotiate agreements, or
learn any sexual skills. Intent upon rebelling against parental
authority and getting out of the house, we unconsciously fall in
love and marry someone who is a duplicate of one or both parents
whom we were desperately trying to get away from.

Informed people approach the arts with the understanding that
it will take at least ten years to master any art form. Yet when it
comes to sexuality, it's supposed to just happen magically. Unless
they're famous, most heterosexuals have limited access to prospec-
tive partners as they struggle through their sex lives with trial and
error. It would be ideal if men and women could experience different kinds of sex with a variety of partners in order to explore a
broader range of their sexuality before they made a commitment.
Today, many of the twenty-something set have only been sexual
with one or two partners before getting married. A similar analogy
would be choosing your favorite food after eating in only two
restaurants—McDonald's and Taco Bell.

As a woman, I had to unravel sex from love, marriage, and security before I could understand how intrinsically they were bound
together. In the seventies, when my career was going well enough
to give me a modest income, I began enjoying sex with different
men without angling for marriage and financial security. It soon

THE VALENTINE. *This young romantic couple is living inside a fairy tale of love everlasting. She is focused on her diamond ring, which symbolizes security. He is pleased to have her as his helpmate to support his future success.*

became clear that what in the past I had called "falling in love" was really about "falling in lust." When the sex was good, I suddenly got busy convincing myself it was because I was in love. When I was in love, I wanted to get married to secure, or "nail down," the relationship. It wasn't until I was able to separate love from sex that I began to fathom either one.

Eventually I was able to make a distinction between the different kinds of love I'd experienced. I know there are endless subtle shades to love, but this was my starting point to better understand this extremely powerful emotion that had for the most part ruled my entire life. Yet I had never defined the word or given it much thought. Love just was.

ROMANTIC LOVE

This is the love that's about being in love with love and idealizing my beloved. This kind of love dominated the decade of my twenties and returned the moment I got divorced. I never really saw the man I claimed to love. Instead, I loved my fantasy of who I wanted him to be. Although sexual fulfillment or the promise of it was part of the early stages of each affair, the emotions of loving love dominated. We were always exclusive, two against the world. I demanded sexual fidelity as proof of his love and he promised to be faithful. Jealousy was a natural part of being in love. I was completely justified in throwing jealous fits of rage when I suspected that he might be attracted to another woman. The degree of my jealousy actually demonstrated the depth of my love; therefore, he could be manipulated through guilt while I withheld sex to punish him. Our emotional arguments and fights only fanned the flames of passionate sex when we made up.

Although my vision for our future was getting married and living happily ever after, these romantic affairs rarely lasted more than a few years because reality eventually eroded my illusions. These affairs were always sexually hottest during the first year. As our sexual exchange cooled down and the arguments heated up, I made every effort to change each lover back into my idealized image, but no matter how hard I tried, I failed. Reality would wake me from my romantic dream. The inevitable breakup had its own brand of sweet sorrow and painful suffering. Eventually I learned to move along to the next beloved without killing myself off with sorrow and regrets.

My marriage was a perfect example of loving love. Since our sexual exchange was never that good, both my husband and I took loving love to new heights. We dipped in and out of the presexual stages of romantic love with both of us being very affectionate and speaking of love while sleeping together without sex. Thanks to the promise my therapist made, I clung to the false hope that after we made our "marital adjustment," our marriage would break out into longer sessions of passionate fucking so I could also have an orgasm, but love without sex continued to rule.

EROTIC LOVE

This kind of love is grounded in my body with physical and sensual pleasures at the center of the relationship. Erotic means the love of sex. Each partner appreciates the other while relishing the joy of mutual sexual gratification. Sexual love serves no other master than pleasure. My erotic lovers and I are inclusive. He or she can be married and either one of us can be sexually intimate with other people. Neither one of us expects the affair to last forever; it simply lasts for as long as it's good. Erotic love can be a joyful part of life for an hour, a night, a week, a month, or for many years. It thrives in the present moment without projecting a future of togetherness. Don't hold your breath waiting for puritanical Americans to ever accept loving sex for the sake of sex, because everyone will be desperately searching for love.

In the past, the French sustained erotic love by separating it from marriage. Mademoiselle married a man for security and children, while she had her lovers for sex. We are one of the few societies that expects sex and passion to be a natural part of marriage, although it rarely is. Today it's acceptable for European married men to openly have mistresses and some wives still have their lovers. The French people knew all about and casually accepted President François Mitterrand's mistress, who openly attended his funeral.

MARITAL LOVE

This kind of love has many faces. With day-to-day living, sexual passion inevitably fades to one degree or another. Some people continue loving love as they idealize the memories of those early romantic times. Other couples get divorced, fall into romantic love and marry again, and again like Liz Taylor and Larry King. However, it takes money to pull that one off. Some married men have sexual flings while others go for long-term extramarital affairs. These men get to have their cake and eat it, too—romantic flings with hot sex along with the respectable cover story of marriage that is required for the public image of politicians and corporate CEOs. A few liberated husbands and wives agree to have brief affairs with no intentions of ever ending their marriage.

Married couples that remain monogamous and stay together after romance fades can either have an intimate friendship with comfortable sex, a warm friendship with affection and minimal sex, or a distant, cool truce with no sex. Those couples that maintain a conflict-habituated marriage by fighting can stir up enough emotion to have hot sex in the process of making up occasionally. When couples say their partnersex keeps getting better after fifty years of marriage, they are either the exception that proves the rule or they have always had very modest sex.

Contrary to popular belief, falling in love doesn't automatically beget good sex. Lovers have to make an effort to learn about each other's bodies, minds, histories, and how they want to share their lives. They need to discover how they each create their own orgasms with self-loving, as well as share a few fantasies to learn about the other's deepest erotic desires. Without this intimate knowledge, partnersex is a superficial process that is about posing, pleasing, or proving, never about enjoying sexual pleasure.

Still, there is no guarantee that even the most skilled of lovers having the best sex imaginable will stay together for a lifetime. In spite of wedding vows and commitment ceremonies, the truth remains that a partnership lasts for as long as it's good. Couples can stay together for the sake of the children or for their careers. They can live together without sharing sex—some masturbate, others have affairs, and many abandon an erotic life altogether. There is no law that says couples must continue to enjoy their sexuality together, alone, or with others.

After several decades of listening to people tell me the intimate details of their sex lives, I can safely say the idea of two people living under the same roof and sharing everything is daunting. It's asking too much of most humans; yet the romantic myth of a lifetime of togetherness with endless hot sex continues to rule the American imagination. There is far less sexual pleasure going on in relationships and marriages than people care to admit. It's as though we are a nation of sexually immature adults who refuse to give up believing in Santa Claus. The Disney Studios will see to it that our dreams of romantic love stay intact as each generation starts their conditioning with a re-release of *Sleeping Beauty* or *Snow White*.

The song may say that love and marriage go together like a horse and carriage, but smart people know sex and money make the world go round. And what about love? As much as we worship the idea of it, love more often hurts than heals. Love causes emotional distress. Love leads to unwanted pregnancies. Love consistently turns into its opposite—hate. There is a lot of violence going down in the name of love: jealous rages between lovers, spouse battering, parents abusing children, and friends fighting with each other. People not only live for love, they die for love, and they also kill for love. Men go to war for love of country and religious wars are waged for love of God.

Just as the Eskimos have different words for snow, we could use different words for the various kinds of love: parental love, marital love, sisterly love, brotherly love, friendship love, erotic love, and, of course, romantic love.

Instead of assuming all forms of love are the romantic variety, it would clear up a lot of confusion if a person said "I lust for you," which would be erotic love. Or if someone said "I want to live with you for my lifetime," which would be marital love. When a mother says "I love you" to a child, it is unconditional love, not the possessive romantic kind. Unrequited love would be seen as "safe love"

since it never becomes sexual. And what about love that turned out
to be friendship with sex? That would certainly put a dent in our
desperate need to have exclusive romantic affairs that feed off possessiveness, jealousy, and insecurity. Love between friends might
climb to the top of the charts as the most cherished kind of love
once we stopped searching for our other halves in the so-called
effort to be whole or to feel complete.

I'm reminded of Plato's allegory: The gods created humans who
were both male and female combined with four arms, four legs,
and both sex organs. But when they saw that their creations had
become so powerful that they were losing control, the gods cut
them in half. That's why to this day people are doomed to constantly search for their "other halves." The idea that there is no such
thing as a whole person makes this a depressing tale. However, it
does clearly show how our romantic notions of love and being
paired off make us helplessly codependent.

Are we a nation of unconscious "romantic love junkies" who,
like Plato's allegory, feel insecure unless our other half is constantly
reassuring us that we are lovable? Regardless of the fact that therapists everywhere tell their clients they have to love themselves
before they can ever love another, people continue to struggle with
the idea. Is self-love so difficult? Could it be that we all have such
low self-esteem that the prospect of loving ourselves is unthinkable?
Do we need to be loved by someone in order to feel validated?

The Bible admonishes us to love our neighbor as we love ourselves. Assuming all people are capable of loving themselves is like
a bad joke, given that religion is most often the source of human
shame, guilt, and self-loathing. According to most organized religions, we're all repeat sinners when it comes to sexuality. On top
of all that, we have to cope with the religious cult of romantic love.

In "Love," an article I admired, Michael Crichton wrote:

> Most of the people I know confuse love with possession. It's easy
> to understand why; it's built into the fundamental assumptions of

our culture. "You're mine," says the popular song, "and we belong together." Hardly anyone stops to question the sentiment.

As soon as we feel love, we immediately attempt to possess. We speak confidently of *my* boyfriend, *my* wife, *my* child, *my* parent. We feel justified in holding expectations about those people. We consider that perfectly reasonable.

Why? Because all our concepts of love ultimately derive from romantic love—and romantic love is furiously, frantically possessive. We want to be with our lover, to have him or her to ourselves, to *possess*. So strongly do we equate love with possession that we may even feel that if someone doesn't want to possess us, he or she doesn't really love us. Yet I would argue that what we call romantic love isn't love at all. It's a kind of emotional storm, an overpowering, thrilling attraction—but it isn't love.

Real love isn't possessive. It can't be. Love involves giving, not taking.

We would all benefit from spending some quality time thinking about how we define and use the word "love," especially since we are avoiding it at all costs, pursuing the dream of it, or deluding ourselves that we have it. Don't get me wrong; I'm still a romantic love junkie. However, I now have periods of clarity when I am able to be in the moment and not to project my expectations of romance onto my partner. Those periods allow me to see love as some form of action—affection, consideration, appreciation, generosity, and, most important, understanding. Whether it's romantic, erotic, familial, or friendship, the idea of love becomes more real when I remember it's a collection of momentary acts rather than a constant state of grace.

❧ 4 ❧

THE BRIDAL SHOWER

We Haven't Come a Long Way, Baby

THE E-MAIL ASKED IF I would be available to give a sex lecture to a group of women at a bridal shower who were all in their twenties. Immediately I thought, "What a great idea." Kitty, the young woman who contacted me, said they considered having a male stripper at first, but that had been done so often. She and her girlfriend Brenda wanted something different. They both decided that having me would be fun as well as informative. Their offer came through my website, so neither one knew anything about me except the opening statement that ended with the sentence: "Join me for an honest, intelligent, and fun-loving exchange of ideas and images about my favorite subject, SEX."

As we talked, I proposed bringing a few sex toys that would enhance women's orgasms alone and with partnersex. I'd also bring some drawings of the female genitals with diagrams of the inner structure, and a dildo to demonstrate how to give a good blowjob. Kitty was thrilled with my proposal. We agreed on an hourly fee and I said the chances were pretty good it would last for three hours.

On Saturday, June 1, 2001, at eight P.M., I showed up at an East Side apartment with my bag of goodies. The room was filled with about twenty or so women who were all young, well-dressed, attractive New York professionals. There is nothing I like better than interacting with younger men and women to find out what they are thinking about in the new millennium. My first assumption was that these generation-Xers would be fairly sexually sophisticated, especially living in New York City.

My opening remark—"Your oversexed grandmother has arrived"—elicited only a few smiles. The rest of them weren't sure how to respond. After all, older women with white hair weren't supposed to be having sex. Kitty, the bright-eyed hostess, bubbled with enthusiasm as she welcomed me and introduced me to the other women. She showed me to a comfortable chair with a small end table in front of it.

As I placed the Magic Wand vibrator, a small battery-operated vibrator, and my Vaginal Barbell on the table, I begin by asking if they were all proficient masturbators. There was an outburst of hysterical laughter and no show of hands. Maybe they were laughing at the size of the electric vibrator, so I quickly explained it was meant to vibrate our sweet little clits. More laughter, but I didn't stop. The best way to use a vibrator for masturbation was with a folded washcloth. When they used it with a partner, I recommended putting a washcloth over the top and holding it in place with a rubber band from a bunch of broccoli. They screamed with laughter.

Looking around the room, I realized only a few women were able to make eye contact with me. The future bride kept her gaze intently on the floor. Others were whispering in private conversations with the woman sitting next to them.

Finally Kitty asked why guys always wanted to watch their girl-friends masturbate? Why would she want to do herself when she had a boyfriend? After all, getting her off was his job, not hers. After lightheartedly accusing her of being a "do me, do me" girl, I said maybe men wanted to see how their girlfriends handled their clits so they'd learn something. The same was true for men. A woman could ask her boyfriend to do himself so she would know what he liked. Sharing masturbation was a great way to learn about each other's sexual response. Besides, it's very hot for a couple to watch each other!

Again the room filled with more howls of laughter. At that point I knew it was going to take awhile to break through the embarrassment, so I became a bawdy comedian, letting them laugh themselves silly. I dived into the pond of heterosexual romantic love, acutely aware of the absence of sexual knowledge that fills it.

Moving ever upward and onward, I passed out Betty's Barbell, a resistance device that I'd designed and manufactured to work the vaginal muscles. It was made of stainless steel and doubled as a fab-ulous dildo. After a few women felt the weight of it, someone finally asked why it was so heavy. That's when I explained that the weight kept it from shooting out of the vagina while a woman tightens her PC muscle. After talking about how to locate the mus-cle, I said that all women would benefit from doing the exercise with the Barbell in place while using some form of stimulation on the clitoris.

Looking at the two pregnant women in the room, I told them their doctors would tell them to do Kegel exercises after giving birth. Actually, a well-toned pelvic floor muscle makes having a baby easier as well as improves a woman's orgasm. One expectant mother said she was already doing her Kegels.

Next I asked if they had all examined their pussies in a mirror with a bright light while using both hands to explore inside and out. Looks of embarrassment combined with more nervous laugh-ter. A few shook their heads. Kitty said several of them had gone to

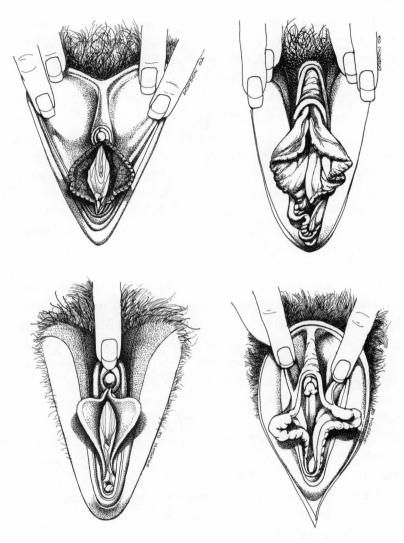

VULVA VARIATIONS. *The longer extended inner lips have caused distress for many women who believed they were somehow genitally deformed. I refer to vulvas with elaborate drapery for inner lips as Baroque or Renaissance style. The vulvas with symmetrical inner lips like petals might have inspired the Art Deco period. We all recognize the heart-shaped vulva, which is probably the real reason lovers celebrated St. Valentine's Day.*

get pussy trims at a salon on 57th Street that she had recommended. They were all perfectly willing to discuss whether they had a bikini wax or they were completely nude, but when I asked if they'd seen their clitorises or knew what type of inner lips they had, no one had any idea. One woman asked, "What are inner lips?"

Out came my book. I opened it up to the pages with the vulva drawings and passed it around. Then I explained how our sex organs are like our faces, with different shapes of noses, eyes, and mouths. Every pussy is as unique as our fingerprints—a significant revelation. When I talked about different genital styles like Classical, Baroque, Renaissance, and Art Deco, several wanted to know which style guys liked the best. I said the ones that had a hole for penetration. This time I joined in the laughter that was becoming more genuine than nervous.

Brenda, who was sitting to my left, wanted to know why it was so difficult to come during intercourse. Perfect question. I asked the group how many of them could have orgasms from fucking only. A sprinkling of hands rose, including Kitty's. When I asked her what position she used, I halfway expected her to say woman on top. Instead she said missionary position. Then I asked if she was aware of what was getting her off while they were fucking? Her explanation was clear that it was a grinding motion when she and her boyfriend pressed up against each other's bodies. The next question was whether she thought she was getting indirect clitoral stimulation. She had no idea.

A great segue into my well-loved clitoral rap. How the clitoris is a woman's primary sex organ, with eight thousand nerve endings, and the vagina is the birth canal. Although sisters Jennifer and Laura Berman state in their book *For Women Only* that 80 percent of women do not orgasm from intercourse alone, I suspected the number was closer to 90 percent if we factored in all the women faking orgasm. While a wet pussy provides ideal direct stimulation for a penis, a woman also needs some form of direct stimulation from her boyfriend's fingers or tongue, or her fingers. If she was accustomed to using a vibrator, she could also use it during intercourse.

One of the women asked if maybe that was why she could only have an orgasm with oralsex. Several nodded in agreement. One woman asked when I was going to demonstrate how to do oralsex on a man, and several others nodded in agreement. We had just started discussing female sexual pleasure and already they wanted to know how to please a man. The female role is connected to such ancient programming that it must be encoded in our cellular structure: How can I please him so he'll kill a wooly mammoth and bring it back to the cave to feed the children and me?

Reaching into my bag, I pulled out a Cyberskin realistic dildo with a suction cup on the bottom. Licking the base, I stuck it onto the small end table in front of me. Everyone in the room gasped at the full eight inches of dick except for one woman who said it looked just like her boyfriend's penis. Then I explained that the average-size penis was around five and a half to six inches erect. The standard is always bigger is better when dildos are manufactured or men are cast in X-rated videos. Yet if the truth were known, most women prefer an average-size penis. It's a shame that so many men are obsessed with penis size, believing their dicks are too small or somehow inadequate. Too bad more men don't realize how few women can orgasm from a penis anyway.

At that point, a woman who had been continuously turning red, gasping, and covering her face finally spoke up. She admitted how embarrassed she'd been in the beginning, but now she wanted to thank me. In the last hour she'd learned more about sex than she had during her entire lifetime. Then she admitted that at twenty-eight she'd never had an orgasm. I assured her she was not alone and advised her to start masturbating so she could learn about her sexuality. Then a woman named Carol joined in, saying she'd never had an orgasm with a partner but she could give herself one. These are magic moments of freeing oneself with the truth. I recom-

mended they both go to my website and get all the necessary information on how to proceed.

My cocksucking demo started with the information that every
man is different, just like every woman. A smart lover asks what his
or her partner likes. Some men prefer a very light stroke while others want a firm grip. It all depends on how he masturbates. As I
spoke, I covered my hands with massage oil and started demonstrating different hand strokes. The laughter and voices talking all
at once were causing quite a din in the room. Even I had to admit
that watching a grandmother doing a dick with style was pretty
outrageous. Yet I also knew I was a well-needed reminder that sex
doesn't end for every woman after she turns fifty, sixty, or seventy.

Continuing, I said a woman's mouth and lips are hot to watch
but most men need more stimulation to come, so it makes sense to
combine hand and mouth. Of course, any woman who is skilled at
doing deep throat will drive her boyfriend to untold heights of
pleasure. One voice asked, "What's 'deep throat'?" Again I'd
assumed too much; I explained that it was when a woman "swallowed" or took a man's penis all the way down her throat. The way
to learn how to do it was by accepting the gag reflex and learning
to relax into it. I was willing to show them what it looked like to
gag and relax, but they all thought it sounded too gross. None of
them wanted to know another thing about deep throat.

Poor Linda Lovelace, the star of the porn movie *Deep Throat,* so
famous in the seventies, was like dust on the Bible. Even the movie
All the President's Men, which used the term "deep throat" for the
informant during the Watergate scandal, was not familiar to this
generation. My, how times change.

Next Brenda asked what female ejaculation was all about. No
longer making assumptions, I asked if anyone had read *The G-Spot.*
None of them had even heard of it. Kitty said she'd read in a
woman's magazine, *Glamour* or *Cosmo,* that female ejaculation was
definitely not urine. It was more like the fluid that came from a
man's prostate gland.

Most young women today are getting their sex misinformation from women's magazines, in articles written by young, sexually inexperienced writers who get their information from experts who are basically talking about what they have read in books or tested with a Ph.D. thesis that relied on a questionnaire. As one of those sex experts, I am constantly being misunderstood and misquoted in magazine articles. Is it any wonder that sexual myths and out-dated information is so rampant?

When I asked how many women had ever experienced ejaculation, two out of twenty raised their hands. Brenda was convinced ejaculation came from her vagina. The other one said her former boyfriend loved it, but she thought it was weird, so with her new lover she didn't do it. Before launching into an explanation, I asked both of them what kind of sex they were having when they squirted.

Brenda said she had to stimulate a pinpoint spot and it only happened during masturbation. At first I thought she was using some G-spot toy, but it turned out she only stimulated her clitoris with a battery-operated vibrator. The pinpoint spot was on her clit, not inside her vagina. It had only happened a few times.

Mary, the other woman, said she ejaculated when her ex-boyfriend used his fingers to rub really hard inside her vagina. When I asked how often ejaculation had occurred, she said it happened all the time with her ex, but now her new lover only uses his fingers to stimulate her clitoris. The final question was if wet orgasms were any better than dry orgasms? They both said no, not necessarily.

Getting out the diagrams from *A New View of a Woman's Body,* I showed them the internal structure of the clitoris and the drawing that showed a model's finger inside her vagina pressing up on the ceiling into the urethral sponge. The sponge protected the urinary tract from getting irritated from the friction of a penis moving in and out of the vagina. Inside the sponge is a small paraurethral gland, which led some to speculate that's where the fluid came from. It had been established that the fluid exits the ure-thra, not the vagina. One study in which female ejaculators were catheterized concluded the fluid was dilute urine and it came from the bladder.

The whole room went crazy over the thought that female ejac-ulation might be urine. That was disgusting! However, when they thought it was prostatic fluid similar to male ejaculate, it was desir-able because it demonstrated that a woman's level of sexual arousal was so high that it made her "come" like a man. That's why "female ejaculators" repeatedly state, "It doesn't smell or taste like urine." The idea of enjoying urinating during sex was a filthy, dirty, nasty idea, while ejaculation sounded sexy.

To allow for the few women who might have fluid emission during orgasm, I explained as long as a woman has a strong PC muscle, and she isn't bearing down, forcing it to happen, squirting is simply a part of her orgasm. I added that there are also some cou-ples who enjoy peeing for fun and there was no need to judge them for their sexual preference.

By then the Barbell had made the rounds, so I discussed the importance of exercising the PC, or pubococcygeal, muscle. First I described how to locate the muscle by stopping the flow of urine or inserting a finger inside the vagina and squeezing the muscle on it. Then I had everyone do several rounds of squeeze and release, telling them that a strong PC muscle would enhance their orgasms. Their boyfriends would also feel them gripping his penis with their muscular vaginas during partnersex. They liked that idea a lot.

We took a break to refill our drinks while Kitty served cake. Ellen, the bride to be, began opening all her presents. It was the usual fare, with sexy lingerie, a few gag gifts, a couple of feather boas, and a book for her wedding photos. I told her she could choose any one of the toys I'd brought as a wedding present from me. She chose the Cyberskin dildo. When I asked if she intended to fuck her husband on their wedding night, we all broke up laugh-ing, including Ellen, and we made good eye contact for the first time. Later on, she changed her mind and decided to take the small battery vibrator instead. Of course, I thought that was a much better choice. I told her clitoral stimulation rather than vaginal penetration takes most of us a lot farther, sexually speaking. Best of all is the combination of both.

As we sat around talking informally, I discovered that Ellen and her boyfriend had been living together for the past four years. They had made a decision not to have sex for a whole month just before they got married to make their wedding night special. One married woman reminded her that they would be too tired to have sex after the wedding ceremony. They'd probably wait and make love the next day.

Since I'd been writing about marriage and monogamy, out of curiosity, I asked Ellen what she'd do if she ever caught her husband cheating. She said she'd get a divorce immediately. It had already happened once since they'd been together, and he'd vowed it would never happen again. Here were two adorable twenty-something kids with a minimum of experience with other people, yet monogamy was an ironclad rule.

Again, out of curiosity, I asked the women what was the favorite kind of birth control these days. There were only two—the pill and condoms. Several of the women who were living with their boyfriends were still using condoms. They had no idea they were missing the exquisite sensation of a bare penis moving inside a slippery vagina, but what you haven't experienced you can't miss. I told them that as a sex educator, I was dedicated to safe sex, but believe me, if I had a choice, condoms would be at the bottom of my list. The pill fucks around with our hormones, so I'd use a diaphragm and agree to be fluid-bonded. The diaphragm was now a birth control fossil and no one knew the term "fluid-bonded."

My explanation was that any woman on the pill, using a diaphragm, or who was postmenopausal made an agreement with her partner not to exchange any bodily fluids (especially semen) with another person. If either of them ever had sex outside their pairbond, they promised to always use a condom. I emphasized that this arrangement required total trust and honesty. These young women saw monogamy as a fact of life, so the possibility that either they or their boyfriend might want to have sex outside the relationship didn't exist.

Looking back, I remember feeling exactly the same way when I was in my twenties, but neither I nor my partner was ever totally successful at being faithful. Cheating was an excuse to break up to find a new, more exciting lover.

After saying good-bye with hugs and kisses, I walked home thinking about how these women's lives were different from mine at the same age. In the fifties as well as the sixties, a woman had to choose between having a career and raising a family. During the seventies and eighties, women were told they could have it all, which meant holding down two full-time jobs—a career and motherhood. The "have it all" generation waited until they were well into their thirties to have babies.

The two women who were pregnant at the shower planned on going back to work eventually, but they intended to spend some quality time raising one or more children. Was honoring motherhood a new trend for generation-X? I certainly hoped so. Raising a child well just might be one of the most creative of all art forms, and it needed to be a conscious commitment not an accident.

Another thing different from my generation was that many of us married our high school sweethearts because serial monogamy wasn't an option. When I moved to New York City at twenty, everyone back home assumed I would end up a prostitute if I didn't get married the first year. Back in the fifties, any woman who had more than one or two sex partners was considered a whore, and living with a man before marriage was living in sin. The married women at the party had all lived with their boyfriends before they made it official, and several of the single women were currently living with their boyfriends. That was one of the big differences.

However, many of the old sexual myths prevailed—women having their orgasms from penis/vagina sex, men keeping their promises to be monogamous, and living happily ever after in marital bliss. Although these women were all computer literate and they lived in one of the most sophisticated cities in the world, traditional romance, love, and marriage was still everyone's favorite sexual fantasy.

All those college courses, books, videos, movies, and the Internet hadn't made much of a dent in female sexuality since the fifties. At least growing up in Kansas I saw dogs, cats, rabbits, and horses fucking. That alone gave me some awareness of the raw power of sex. These city girls had access to a lot more sexual information than I did, but in terms of developing sexual skills and being knowledgeable about their own bodies and orgasms, they were not that much farther along.

In other words, we hadn't come a long way, baby. Our so-called new information age wasn't getting through on the sexual level. Each new generation still has to rediscover the wheel all over again. We wonder why there is so much violence in America, yet so few have the courage to embrace its opposite—sexual pleasure.

Still, I had to give these young women credit. Having a sex educator at a bridal shower was one of the smartest ideas I'd ever heard of. Two of Kitty's friends wanted to hire me for an upcoming shower, so I have a new career if I want one. Just about the time I think I'm ready to chill out with a little time to putter, the phone starts ringing off the hook again. Since oversexed grannies are fairly rare these days, it looks as if I'm going to continue to be in great demand. Although I'm always complaining about having so many projects to complete, I'd rather be busy than bored.

✣ 5 ✣

LOVING OTHERS

Defusing the Power Struggle

T HE DAY I GOT MARRIED, the minister asked my husband if he would promise to love, honor, and *cherish* me.
I was then asked if I would love, honor, and *obey* him. The
ceremony ended with, "I now pronounce you man and wife." He
was still himself while I had the new title of "wife," a role that
would change my very identity, complete with a new last name.
When two people fall in love they become one—the problem is
which one.

This ongoing power struggle exists in most marriages unless
one partner or the other takes the traditional role of the dutiful
wife. While it's true that some women are happy with a subordinate position, that doesn't mean this dynamic will work for all of
us. A few couples have a role reversal where the husband defers to
his wife—a widespread but rarely mentioned marital dynamic that

society pretends doesn't exist because it's not considered appropriate behavior. A relatively recent role for a man is househusband. A few men are happy staying at home caring for the children while their wife goes off to the office. Some couples both bring in an income and they share household chores and child care, but it's never completely equal, so they still have their power struggles, maybe just a little bit less.

I will never forget, after we were married, the early stage of playing the role of "His Wife." One day I'd spent hours cleaning every inch of the apartment. That evening, my husband came home to a beautifully set table with dinner simmering on the stove à la *Good Housekeeping.* He didn't seem to notice, so I joyfully pointed out my domestic masterpiece. He went over to a window and ran his finger over the top of the sash and showed me the dirt I'd missed. A white-hot rage shot through me. I'd seen some jackass of a man do that in a movie. Something snapped inside me and I was awakened from my "Happily Married" dream.

After many arguments about the housework being my responsibility because he earned the money, I finally said, "Bullshit!" I worked every day in my art studio, and from now on we would be sharing the housework. His annoying habit of leaving his shoes on the living room floor ended when I put them in the freezer. By the end of our first year, any resemblance to a traditional marriage had vanished. My demands for equality didn't help our already troubled sex life, which eventually disappeared, too. Ours was a marriage doomed to fail when I scratched my seven-year itch.

What I used to call "sex roles" has now become "gender roles." Both terms describe the social activities we are expected to perform as women and men. For the most part, these roles are taken for granted, so they're seldom noticed unless someone crosses over into the opposite role. My friend Veronica Vera, who wrote the book *Miss Vera's Finishing School for Boys Who Want to Be Girls,* has one of the best explanations of the differences between society's stringent boundaries for sex roles and the term "gender" that I've come across. Veronica said that in the recent past, the prevalent thinking was a person's sex organ and sexual identity was one and the same. The idea that a person could change his or her sexual identity was unheard of until 1952, when George Jorgensen underwent surgery and became Christine.

About the same time, Dr. John Money borrowed the term "gender" from its original use in English and coined the terms "gender roles" and "gender identity" to use for his work at Johns Hopkins, the first American hospital to perform sex change surgery. He became a gender god, turning baby boys with teeny penises into girls and surgically removing big clitorises on baby girls. Along with a thriving community of transvestites (cross-dressers) and transsexuals (people who've had sex change operations), we have a politically active group of intersexuals (people with ambiguous genitals) who want to stay the way they are born.

It's no surprise that not all men and women are content to be limited by what society calls "normal" masculine or feminine behavior determined by our genitalia. Any person who does not conform to these socially constructed roles is now said to be suffering from "gender dysphoria." At Miss Vera's Finishing School, gender dysphoria becomes "gender euphoria." A man who identifies as male in everyday life gets to take a vacation from masculinity to explore his feminine side, allowing him to become more of a whole person. Many cross-dressers are heterosexual, while others are gay or bisexual. The same is true for women who want to dress as men.

When I broke away from the traditional female role in the mid-seventies, I spent a period of time with a shaved head and wearing army fatigues and boots. Passing as a little guy was an incredible experience in terms of how differently people behaved toward me. I was waited on faster in restaurants, treated more seriously in general, given more physical space in public, and men no longer hit on me or did the usual wolf whistling. Once I got cruised by a gay man, but even then, he was more direct and honest than the usual heterosexual man hungrily ogling a chick.

The androgyny that I so loved in the seventies is making a comeback. I've been told that some college students are using the terms "heteroflexible" and "homoflexible." A group of young women who are going to school at NYU told me they were LUGs—lesbians until graduation. I see all of this as very positive. Blurring the differences between the sexes will provide more equal opportunities in other areas. We will all have more social and sexual freedom once we become gender fluid.

The truth is we are all androgynous, with both masculine and feminine traits, including genes, cells, chromosomes, and hormones. In the womb, men's sex organs develop from the female sex organs. We can play many roles and enjoy a much broader range of erotic delights beyond the two dimensional "Me Tarzan, you Jane" with what is considered "normal" heterosexual penis/vagina intercourse. The different sex roles women and men play are not "natural," but socially constructed.

My first conscious feminist sex role was choosing to be a *bachelor,* as I claimed the same sexual freedom single men had always enjoyed. Other feminists rejected my idea of sexual liberation and accused me of being "male identified." As a sexual libertarian, I ignored the matriarchal feminists. Once I realized I could design my sex life with the same creative process I used to paint a picture, many sex roles followed. When asked my sexual preference, I'd often answer, "I'm a work in progress."

After menopause, I wanted to try something new and different sexually. A friend of mine belonged to an SM group of lesbian and bisexual women who viewed sex as a conscious exchange of power between two or more adults. Intrigued, I joined the group. We dressed for sex, played with dominance and submission, used erotic bondage, and comingled intense sensations with pleasure. What a revelation for an idealist like myself, who was still struggling with the belief that there could be love between equals.

In most gay or straight relationships, one partner is dominant and the other subordinate. I just couldn't see it. Even when couples switch back and forth, the power structure of top and bottom remains to a degree. Actually, it's quite practical. When two people are both bottoms, nothing much happens sexually because no one makes the first move. If they are both tops, partnersex can become similar to a wrestling match to see who gets pinned first and who has to say "uncle" before they can get around to having orgasms.

Once a couple consciously chooses to play different roles, it's very liberating as well as a lot of fun. Eric and I have been sharing a variety of roles since we've been living together. When it comes to the different roles based on the nuclear family, we take turns doing them all. He's a wonderful mother figure, making sure I take care of myself. Every so often he's my daddy. Eric is an only child, while I grew up with three brothers. Sometimes he's my son, my little brother, or my older brother. I am the little sister he never had, his mommy, and also his grandmother.

We agree that I'm the boss when it comes to running the business, but we also agree that this role gets mixed up with "mother" when I'm telling him what to do. So there is still a power struggle going on when we are working together. I understand that his resentments stem from being raised by an authoritarian mom the same as I was. The thankless role of being a mother giving children orders is universal. My style of leadership is often similar to that of a domineering mother who is critical. I'm working on becoming a wise grandmother who praises her grandchild instead of criticizing him constantly. Since I don't bake cookies, I make it a point to reward Eric by taking him out to his favorite restaurant once a week.

We take turns being teacher and student. Eric came to me with many sexual skills, and I had a wealth of experience. This combination has enabled us to discover a lot about partnersex together.

We constantly experiment with positions and try out different angles for penetration and clitoral stimulation. Since he has so much testosterone and youthful energy, he usually initiates sex and I often bottom for him. I have more social skills and he's learning about interacting with other people from me.

As roommates, we have agreed on how we share the work around the apartment without the traditional division of labor. He's better in the kitchen than I am, but I have the responsibility of seeing to it that the next batch of distilled water is steamed for drinking because he kept forgetting. He thinks I have OCD (obsessive-compulsive disorder) with my need to have everything in its place, while I'm convinced he's got IFD ("I forgot" disorder) when he doesn't remember to put things back.

Our intergenerational relationship allows us to be very light-hearted and playful. Hands down, our favorite fantasy role-playing is Owner and Puppy. It's a whimsical game that amuses and endears us to each other. When he's my adorable puppy, I am his doting mistress dishing out pure unconditional love and affection. Although I know some people abuse animals, most dog and cat owners know the boundless love that exists between them and their pet. Just as a puppy or kitten opens a normally guarded heart to emotions of tenderness, Eric opens mine when he's my little doggie. For me, the sweetness of unconditional love and the heat of sexual desire is an extraordinary combination that I never experienced before.

The psychosexual dynamics of intergenerational sex has rarely been explored with the woman being the older one who has the power. A large part of our compatibility is based upon the difference in our age, clarity about the exchange of power, and turning the imbalance of power into a delightful game. The challenge I face is similar to that of a husband who earns more money than his wife—not to abuse my power. His challenge is not to manipulate me by being so cute that I always give him his way. Meanwhile, we continue to enjoy playing our Puppy and Owner game privately or with a few close friends. When we are out socially, he is my handsome young assistant.

One night Eric had an attack of IFD and forgot to call and say he'd be home in the morning. He was playing cards with the boys and when it got late he decided to sleep over. We had an agreement that he would always call if he stayed out all night. Worried sick until he showed up, I was furious and wanted nothing more to do with him. I told him he had to move out and refused to talk to him the entire day.

That evening, I was sitting in bed watching television when I heard a soft bark. There he was, naked on all fours with a rose in his puppy mouth looking at me with mournful puppy eyes around the corner of the door to my room. Once again my angry heart melted into unconditional love. Overcome with instant forgiveness, I patted the bed for him to jump in. He curled up beside me and laid his head in my lap. As I petted his dark poodle curls, my anger dissolved. In the past I always had trouble forgiving the men in my life, but I can easily forgive my puppy.

There is no doubt in my mind that all enjoyable partnerships are based on forgiveness, compromise, and acceptance. Psychologists Andrew Christensen and Neil S. Jacobson wrote the book *Reconcilable Differences,* which made a lot of sense. Their approach is that instead of trying to force each other to change, which is what I always did in the past, partners need to begin accepting each other's differences and appreciating their individual personalities and behaviors. The authors of *acceptance therapy* pointed out that when people feel pressure to change, they tend to become defensive and withdraw or they become rebellious. When they feel accepted and understood, they are more likely to change willingly. Acceptance and compassion brings couples closer together.

Here is a perfect example: At first I disliked Eric's habit of leaving the toilet seat up after he peed. For weeks I tried different approaches to get him to put the lid down because it looked more aesthetic. My beginning tactic was to charge him a dollar every time he left the seat up, but that meant I had to keep track by writing it down each time. Eventually that became a drag. My next tactic was to stand in the bathroom and wail like a siren until he came in, clamped his hand over my mouth, and put the lid down. That was fun for a while, but then it, too, got boring. Finally one day I realized that putting the lid down myself was a small price to pay for all the pleasure we shared. After I told Eric the toilet seat no longer mattered, he remembered to put it down more frequently.

One of the biggest power struggles between couples is based upon a desire to possess the one we love. When I was in the traditional female role, monogamy was a given once we had sex and being jealous was natural. Jealousy either reduced me to a sniveling mass of tears or it made me angry and competitive, and I'd think "Okay, two can play this game." The minute I'd see my boyfriend looking at another woman, I'd flirt with every man who crossed our path. But revenge never made me feel better; in fact, I'd end up feeling so mean-spirited that I didn't like myself.

These ongoing suspicious fears that my boyfriend might be sexually attracted to another woman kept me in a state of mental uneasiness as I vigilantly watched his every move when we were socializing. Jealousy caused many violent lovers quarrels with screaming matches, accusations, threats, and tears as I tried to control each lover.

My struggle to learn how to love someone without demanding monogamy dates back to the sixties, when Grant and I first began to explore sex together. Once I was presented with the choice of remaining possessive and having sex with one man at a time or getting beyond jealousy to enjoy sex with multiple partners, I wisely chose sexual abundance over the illusion of security that monogamy is supposed to provide.

The first year I did battle with my jealous feelings was an internal war that I eventually won. The fruits of my emotional struggle were claiming my sexual power and personal identity. I became a whole person instead of half of a couple. Unfortunately, society has little use for a sexually and financially independent woman. We threaten the status quo.

By the time I turned forty, loving another person meant honoring his or her freedom—it wasn't about taking a hostage who had to be guarded day and night to make sure he or she remained my private sexual property. Instead, my lovers and I treated each other more like friends who respected one other's personal integrity and independence. While this might sound as if I'm from another planet, think a moment.

People who love and explore sex are no different from food connoisseurs, dedicated scientists, or other people who devote time to pursuing a particular interest. When I was an artist working long hours painting, I was admired and rewarded. Once I became interested in spending my time pursuing sex, I was labeled "nymphomaniac" or, more recently, "sex addict."

Here comes the part that proves I'm from Earth. After all those years dedicated to honoring people's sexual independence, I was shocked to be thrown back into the raw emotions of jealousy at the beginning of my relationship with Eric. Because of our age difference, I was convinced he'd eventually find a pretty young thing and run off. The thought of losing my recent source of sexual happiness made me so anxious I wanted to get it over with quickly. One moment I was pushing him into the arms of another women only to reel him back in the next. Finally my intelligence kicked in and overpowered my emotions. I stopped trying to control him. Taking away his freedom to choose was a form of abuse, not love.

This time around, my skirmishes with jealousy were far more challenging for several reasons. In the past, my lovers and I had our own apartments, giving us more freedom to live separate lives. Living under the same roof with another person creates a series of comfortable patterns that lead to many more dependencies. Another thing was my age. It was much easier to practice nonmonogamy when I was a handsome forty-year-old woman with many years ahead of me. As a senior, I am looking at the end of my life while Eric is at the beginning of his.

My saving grace is the knowledge that the best way for any intergenerational partnership to thrive is for the older person not to possess the younger one sexually. I've had a phenomenal sex life during a time when everything was safe and available. Eric is just starting out on his sexual journey, and it's my firm belief that experience is essential in mastering any art form, including sex. I want him to enjoy a varied sex life with women of all ages. This is not always easy, but then neither is the democratic process. Civil liberties include a person's right to choose how they practice sex.

For me, jealousy is first felt as anger, then as a cooling down to hurt, and finally, at the bottom, as insecurity and fear of abandonment that probably go back to Daddy. This is maddening because I know the idea of security is one big fat illusion. My recent bouts with jealousy made it clear that I needed to relax the emotional muscle that goes into a spasm, clamping down with negative feelings based upon insecurity. Instead of treating every feeling as a fact that dictates my reality, as an older, wise woman I could choose how I respond.

The moment jealousy creeps into my awareness, I acknowledge the feeling, but I do not allow it to dictate my actions or infringe upon my decision-making process. Feeling guilty or jealous is like a bad habit or an addictive drug. The same as I did when I was coming off any drug, I tell myself I choose to stop. It's similar to withdrawing from cigarettes. Whenever the desire to smoke enters my mind, I say, "I am nicotine free." Then I go over my list of all the reasons why I no longer smoke. The measure of any commitment is the struggle between yes and no and when to choose one over the other.

My antijealousy list goes something like this: Jealousy is a destructive emotion. I have a right to choose sexual abundance over possessiveness. Jealousy only hurts me as well as the person I claim to love. Demanding monogamy is the source of jealousy. Sexual possessiveness is not a cure-all for the fear of loss. Many lose partners through accidental death. Jealousy causes people to harm or even kill one another in the name of love. The idea of having sex with only one person for an entire lifetime is ludicrous for people who see the practice of sex as an art form.

Very few couples will ever consider abandoning monogamy and dealing with the emotional chaos that results from feelings of jealousy. However, I'd like to remind women that monogamy was invented to ensure a man's paternity by sexually controlling our behavior. While all men might agree to be faithful, very few intend to do so or actually succeed. So-called monogamous husbands spend billions of dollars on all forms of sexual entertainment, including mistresses, prostitutes, massage parlors, topless bars, and lap dances. Society meanwhile continues to use wives as the unpaid moral police force responsible for enforcing sexual fidelity.

A friend of mine had been faithful for sixteen years. Just after he turned forty, his horniness spilled over into a one-night stand at a conference. When his wife found a woman's business card in his suit, she confronted him, and because he was consumed with guilt, he confessed. For the next two years his wife punished him by withholding sex and constantly reminding him she could never trust him again. Sound familiar? We tend to forget that as women we can dish out our own brand of sexual abuse. Although we claim our anger is a normal response to "sexual betrayal," we are really wallowing in our righteous indignation. We see other women doing it all the time in movies and television. We've been brainwashed to believe jealousy is a sign of "true love."

One of the reasons men don't speak out openly against monogamy is because many want to maintain the current sexual double standard. While these husbands feel they are entitled to fuck around, they'd never accept their wives' claiming the same freedom. After one monogamous wife of thirty years discovered her husband had been cheating off and on during their marriage, she decided what was good for the goose was good for the gander. Suzanne asked me to coach her through her first extramarital affair. Although she was in her early fifties, she was more like a teenager having sex for the first time. Her only sexual partner had been her husband.

My counsel was the following: As a mature woman, she didn't have to wait any mandatory length of time before having sex. Receiving oralsex would be safe for her partner, but she would need to know a lot more about him to fully reciprocate. Manual sex would be totally safe. When it came to intercourse, she was not to rely on a man having condoms or to assume he would know how to correctly use one. A whole session was devoted to her learning how to put a condom on a dildo and practicing until she could do it with ease. She had an affair with a married man that lasted a year. As it turned out, they never had sexual intercourse. The guy was Catholic and didn't want to cheat on his wife. So they did everything else, which worked fine for her. She found the affair very exciting and looked forward to each of her business trips to Europe until it ended.

Although Suzanne never told her husband about the affair, she did tell him she'd recently learned how to have orgasms with an electric vibrator and wanted to use one when they had sex together. She'd actually been using a vibrator for ten years while hiding it from her husband, convinced he'd be devastated if he found out. Instead, he was thrilled with his newly orgasmic wife, and they had a sexual renaissance.

Even an affair that's kept secret can bring a couple closer together—contrary to what moralists will tell you. We often appreciate our spouses even more after we've been sexual with someone else. The idea or fantasy of having sex with someone new is usually better than the actual experience.

There have been a few groups that have tried to get away from the troubling aspect of owning another person in the name of love. The Oneida community was a religious group whose members were encouraged not to form permanent attachments because it divided the group. Eventually people paired off and it failed. The sixties and seventies had communes that were intentional communities where the members made an effort to get beyond monogamy and to initiate more sexual freedom. Married couples called "swingers" continue to share sex with other couples. More recently there are people who identify themselves as polyamorous. They believe it's possible to sexually love more than one person. Jealousy is still a factor in all of these alternatives.

Nowadays, many people claim the threat of disease is too great a risk and they use the fear of contracting AIDS as a reason or an excuse to be monogamous. Some men and women feel insecure when faced with the idea of having sex with another person for the first time—they like monogamy. Others suspect they are lousy in bed and sex outside the marriage is too threatening—they prefer monogamy. One man said he was monogamous out of laziness.

Since jealousy appears to be as inevitable as war, most couples maintain a "Don't ask, don't tell" policy. This is probably the easiest solution for partners who stray. A girlfriend of mine has a weekend lover and he thinks she's monogamous. He has no idea she's enjoying the occasional sexual fling during the week. Many wives have said they suspect their husband has been unfaithful, but they don't want to know about it. Some women say they don't care if their husband fools around as long as he comes home to them. Other married couples are so angry at each other that neither cares what the other is doing sexually. It's the rare couple that excites each other by describing their extramarital sex in detail, but they do exist.

Whether women control, deny, or express their jealous feelings, my hope is that we will learn to stop glorifying the emotion like it is justified and take an honest look at what we are doing. We have been programmed to cling to jealousy and nurture these devastating feelings of loss and abandonment. Sexual possessiveness and jealousy are not natural, as many assume. Jealousy is a learned response that grows out of the myth of romantic love. We are promised passionate sex with one person who will be exclusively devoted to us throughout our lifetime. Today the only alternative to monogamy is the acceptance of serial monogamy, where people have several or many marriages.

It is my firm belief that jealousy turns into a cancerous growth that eats away at our self-esteem, inner strength, and creativity. For anyone who might be interested in managing the devastating feelings of sexual possessiveness and the ensuing fear of loss, here are a few actions I have taken to heal myself.

1. When jealousy is so intense that it makes me feel physically ill, I masturbate to orgasm and reaffirm my sexual worth with more self-loving.

2. Whenever I feel hurt because I think I'm being left out, I tell my partner how I feel without expressing anger or blame.

3. When my partner's behavior hurts my feelings, instead of upping the ante by hurting back, I remember that revenge, retribution, and getting even is like spitting into a fan and getting it back in my face.

4. When we are walking down the street and my partner ogles a movie-star type, I start cruising others while making comments on how great they look.

5. When I imagine being left for someone else, instead of actually rehearsing the death of our relationship, I return to the present moment and appreciate the joy we are currently sharing.

6. If I think my partner is having more fun than I am, I take a closer look at how I can improve the quality of my life and enjoy myself more.

In view of the fact that the ideal of monogamy will most likely continue to endure or only very gradually change, at the very least, we need to find a way to forgive our loved ones for the occasional sexual transgression. Love has the capacity to let go. Loving others is not about restricting their behavior and then punishing them if they break a moralistic rule that is for the most part unrealistic. That's not about loving someone, it's about controlling them. Maybe the day will come when people's self-love will be sufficient to eliminate sexual pairbondage. Until then, I choose to remain optimistic as I practice nonpossessive sex.

❧ 6 ❧

DID YOU COME?

The Mystery of the Female Orgasm

FEMALE ORGASM HAS BEEN DESCRIBED in countless romantic ballads as well as measured under the bright lights of scientific scrutiny, yet it still remains a mystery. The sexual orgasm is one of my favorite metaphors for life: I have often experienced these heightened moments of pleasure in my body, mind, and soul, yet I can never fully describe what happens with words. I've had some orgasms that are barely perceptible, others felt as good as a sneeze, and then there are those orgasms that have turned me into a quivering mass of utter delight as I transcend space and time, soaring through a star-filled universe. But there I go with another description of orgasm that feeds into the already existing romantic myths.

After four decades of observing women's orgasms socially and professionally, even I have resorted to asking the dreaded question,

"Did you come?" No wonder the same question rests on so many men's lips. One of the reasons women dislike being asked is because many of us do not have orgasm during partnersex. Sometimes the woman herself may not know if she came or, in some cases, she is deliberately faking orgasm. Since men often measure their sexual ability by a woman's response, women who are not orgasmic worry that their lovers might stray. So whether we lie to protect his ego or admit the truth, we feel sexually inadequate.

There is no law that says all women must be orgasmic. Many say they enjoy the affection and closeness of sexual intercourse without a climax. While it's true that an orgasmic woman doesn't have to come every time she has partnersex, if she isn't coming some of the time, she will eventually see intercourse as a tiresome routine. Why is it that something as fundamental as an orgasm continues to elude so many women or become such a long painful process to learn? I believe the answer lies somewhere between the romantic misinformation that falling in love will automatically include orgasmic partnersex, the repression of female masturbation, and women not being taught sexual skills.

The greatest tragedy for women in recent history came about when Dr. Sigmund Freud formulated his theory that the clitoris was an infantile source of pleasure and that once a woman fully submitted to the sexual act, the excitement she once felt in her clitoris would be transferred to the vagina. One might ask how he arrived at this conclusion since he didn't have a clitoris or a vagina. Perhaps Mrs. Freud was faking a few to keep hubby happy. Although he was a brilliant and brave man, Freud's infamous theory has kept countless numbers of women from becoming orgasmic. Despite ample evidence that the clitoris is the source of orgasm for most women, vaginal orgasm as a result of intercourse remains the preferred kind of partnersex to this day.

When I came of age in the fifties, I was desperate to be "sexually mature." That meant phasing out masturbation and going through the tedious process of learning how to come from a man's penis moving inside my vagina. It was no easy matter. After much trial and error and many missed climaxes, I discovered that if I got on top during intercourse and established a rhythm, I could climax *some of the time.* When I found a lover who could sustain an erection for at least fifteen minutes (which wasn't easy), it would still take weeks before I felt secure enough to get on top. At that point he became the source of all of my orgasms. Within a year of two, one of us would fall out of love and we would break up. Once again I would be back to doing "immature" clitoral masturbation.

By the time William Masters and Virginia Johnson hailed the primacy of the clitoris in the sixties, I was already divorced and enjoying intercourse combined with direct manual clitoral stimulation. Masters and Johnson claimed that clitoral and vaginal orgasms were not separate biological entities—regardless of the source of stimulation, all orgasms centered in the clitoris. Then later, amazingly enough, they contradicted their own findings with a description of indirect clitoral stimulation that was so utterly bizarre it degenerated into a modified version of vaginal orgasm. They stated that the thrusting action of the penis exerted traction on the vaginal opening, specifically the inner lips, which caused the hood covering the clitoris to move back and forth, stimulating the head of the clitoris. In the end, Mr. Penis retained the crown as the most legitimate source of a woman's orgasm.

In the sixties, I also discovered the writings of Wilhelm Reich, who had been a student of Freud. In his book *The Function of the Orgasm,* Reich not only describes the process of orgasm but also the necessity of experiencing consistent sexual release. Like Freud, he believed a woman could climax from intercourse if she had a man who was potent. Freud and Reich never got to read the Kinsey report, which put America's national average time of thrusting with full erection after penetration at two and a half minutes. That's barely enough time to get me interested in sex, let alone have an orgasm.

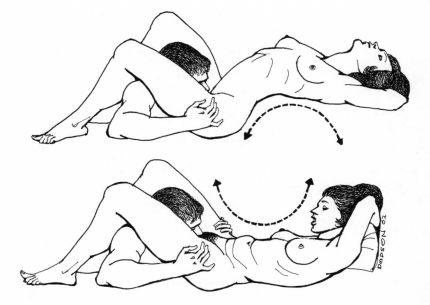

THE HYSTERICAL ARCH. *This position was described by Wilhelm Reich, the well-known sex researcher. Over the years I have often seen this in many women. The arch looks pretty and we often see it portrayed in films and porn. However, when a woman drives her genitals down toward the floor and throws her head back, she literally cuts off much of her genital sensation. The forward thrust, in which the pelvis curls up to embrace clitoral stimulation with the head curving up at the other end, represents a more authentic orgasmic response.*

Although I differed with Reich on the function of the clitoris, I agreed with him on many of his other ideas about orgasm and partnersex. In another one of his books, *The Sexual Revolution,* Reich spoke about "compulsory heterosexuality" and "compulsory monogamous marriage" as problems rather than sacred cows—a very radical concept that totally intrigued me, since I had been questioning both in terms of my own life.

In 1970, the President's Commission on Obscenity and

Pornography recommended the repeal of all laws prohibiting the distribution of sexually explicit materials to consenting adults. The floodgates opened as feminist articles and books started breaking down traditional notions of female sexuality that had been formulated by male researchers. The first article to inspire me to action was "The Myth of the Vaginal Orgasm" written by Anne Koedt. I was so impressed that I made an appointment to see her and get reprints of her article to pass out to all the women in my CR group.

In 1971, my art and sexual views appeared in an interview in *Evergreen,* an avant-garde magazine published by Grove Press. The article was accompanied by a large sampling of my sex drawings, along with positive statements about the importance of masturbation to women's sexual liberation. That led to an editor from the recently formed *Ms.* magazine requesting an article from me on masturbation. When I submitted seventeen pages titled "Liberating Masturbation," the editors feared my views would cause women to cancel their subscriptions. They said they might publish the article at a later date, when they felt the time was right. Infuriated to think feminists had censored me, I published several thousand copies and began distributing the information myself.

While many feminists struggled with my ideas about women's sexual liberation, sex professionals were interested; Ed Brecher, a noted author and sex researcher, was extremely supportive. He agreed that most women could learn to have orgasms through masturbation, and then use that knowledge to become orgasmic with a partner. Wardell Pomeroy, who worked with Alfred Kinsey, and Albert Ellis, who has written hundreds of books on sex, also supported my views on the importance of female masturbation. Alex Comfort was heartbroken when I didn't do the line illustrations for *The Joy of Sex*. However, I did illustrate Helen Kaplan's *The New Sex Therapy*. At the time, Dr. Kaplan headed the sex therapy program at the Payne Whitney Clinic of New York Hospital.

Kaplan came to my studio the day I'd hired a photographer to shoot the sex positions we had discussed. While Grant and I took

the poses naked, Helen directed us to do this and that. After showing her my favorite right-angle position, where I did my own clitoral simulation during intercourse, I gave an impassioned plea for
her to include a drawing of it in her book. The drawing appeared,
but a disclaimer went with it saying a woman stimulates herself to
a point just prior to orgasm *and stops*. She then has her climax from
his penis "thrusting vigorously," thereby having a "coital orgasm."
Kaplan said a woman who needed clitoral stimulation all the way
to orgasm during intercourse didn't necessarily represent a treat-
ment failure, but her bias was crystal clear.

My Secret Garden by Nancy Friday came out in 1973, and
although the content of women's sexual fantasies shocked many,
her book sold millions of copies. Her many informants made it
obvious that women not only masturbated, but they did it with
images that were bawdy and very unladylike. *Ms.* magazine
wouldn't even review Nancy's book, but they finally published a
couple of pages from my original article after having shelved it for
over two years. In response to their heavily edited version, thousands of women wrote in wanting more information about female
masturbation and orgasm.

Unable to find a publisher that would consider doing an entire
book on female masturbation, I published and began distributing
Liberating Masturbation in 1974. Best of all were the sixteen full-page
pen-and-ink "pussy portraits" I did of my friends showing the differences among individual genitals as well as the beauty of women's
sex organs in general. Although my book was considered part of a
feminist underground, I was selling it through the U.S. Post Office.
I claimed that masturbation forever put an end to the concept of
frigidity. If a woman can stimulate herself to orgasm, she is sexually
healthy. "Frigid" is a man's word for a woman who can't have an
orgasm in the missionary position in a few minutes with only the
kind of stimulation that's good for him.

Lonnie Barbach followed in 1975 with her book *For Yourself.* At
one of my early workshops in 1973, she stood in the doorway tak-

ing notes. Since Lonnie was a Ph.D. psychologist, her book helped to legitimize masturbation, but we differed on one important point: I felt masturbation could be an end in itself, and she saw it only as a way for women to learn about orgasm to improve partnersex. She, too, believed in the coital orgasm, or teaching women how to retire a vibrator so they could at least orgasm from a lover's fingers.

The *Hite Report,* which entered the picture in 1976, was a remarkable though not scientific survey of female sexuality. When Shere Hite showed me her involved and complex questionnaire, I urged her to simplify it, saying there was no way women would take the time to write out essay-type answers. I was wrong. The women she contacted through NOW chapters and several magazines couldn't wait to tell the details of their sex lives. Her conclusion that any woman could easily masturbate to orgasm is not true for *all* women then or now. She did not take into account the built-in bias of her survey. Middle- or upper-class white women who liked sex or were interested in the subject were the ones who took the time and trouble to fill out her questionnaire.

Any sex researcher who has the commitment and patience to gather information, run statistics, and then crunch numbers has my undying admiration. However, when it comes to presenting their findings, it's only human that some end up proving their own subjective bias in the name of objective science.

Since my Ph.D. in sexology came much later—at the age of sixty-two—my understanding of female sexuality is primarily experiential and very subjective, with a little objectivity thrown in. Throughout all the years I've taught sex by doing sex, I continue to think of myself as an artist rather than an academic bound by traditional methods of statistical analysis. My strength lies in the respectable research called "working in the field." As a self-proclaimed sexual anthropologist, I've been having sex with the natives in most of the major cities here and abroad. In 1966, when I first began attending sex parties, I was shocked to see how many women were accommodating men and faking orgasms.

Without the need to please a partner, it seems obvious to me that masturbation is a more direct route for women to enjoy pleasurable sensation and orgasms. Therefore how a woman masturbates needs to be translated into partnersex, not the other way around. I know there are some women who do not like direct clitoral stimulation. They start and end with vaginal stimulation, masturbating with a dildo. However, in all my years of observing female sexuality, I never once saw a woman doing clitoral stimulation until she was about to come, then grab a dildo and fuck herself to orgasm.

Although no two orgasms from self-stimulation are exactly alike, most women use some form of direct or indirect clitoral stimulation with or without penetration. The body responds with movement, no movement, and different breathing patterns from panting to holding the breath. Some women remain silent, while others make a variety of sounds. The mind can be paying attention to what a woman is feeling in her body or focused on her sexual thoughts or fantasies. During my workshops, a handful of women looked around the room, while most kept their eyes closed, listening to the sounds. Later I designed a process that allowed them to look at what was happening so they could have images of different women being sexual.

COMMON TYPES OF ORGASM

The following categories are in no way complete. They represent some of the general variations of women's sexual responses that I have observed socially, during my workshops, and in private sessions. I have included my own experiences as well. Many of these observations will also apply to men.

Pressure orgasms are frequently used in childhood with some kind of indirect genital stimulation. We all start off sexual. It has been repeatedly documented with sonograms that both unborn boys and girls engage in genital self-stimulation. From the age of five to around seven years of age, I clearly remember rocking back and forth with a pillow pulled up between my legs to get that "tingly feeling." One workshop woman said she pressed her clitoris against overstuffed furniture; another pressed against the hard nose on her teddy bear. Some little girls squeeze their legs together to get good feelings and a few carry that over into adulthood for their orgasmic release.

Never moving beyond indirect stimulation might make it easier for a woman to climax from intercourse alone. Maybe that's why the clitoris has been denied for so long. Because once a woman has had a more direct form of clitoral contact, she will definitely want more of it. Women who grew up with a strong prohibition about touching themselves directly have made a transition to stronger orgasms by letting the water run on their clitoris from a bathtub faucet. Others say wearing tight jeans got them off, and more than a few were very fond of their bicycle seats. As a preteen, I was crazy about riding horses before I got interested in boys.

Tension orgasms, with direct genital rubbing and muscle tension, get most of us through puberty, into young adulthood, and, for some, through the rest of our lives. Tension orgasms rely on leg and buttock muscles being squeezed tight, with the rest of the body held fairly rigid. While holding the breath, a fast motion is used on the clitoris or penis for a few moments or minutes until orgasm explodes in a quick burst. Because these climaxes are silent, many of us grow up masturbating this way to avoid getting caught by our siblings or parents. These quick tension orgasms often carry over into many men coming quickly in partnersex.

A few women have orgasms with muscle tension only, without any direct genital contact. One woman climaxed by hanging from the top of a door to create tension in her entire body while squeezing her vaginal muscle tight. She had to come in under a minute due to the stress in her arms. In contrast to coming fast, a friend of mine has developed tension orgasms without clitoral contact into an art form. Now in her early fifties, she's in great shape from all the isometric exercise she gets by straining against some form of erotic bondage or keeping her body rigid during elaborate scenes of suspension.

Most people are too busy to spend quality time enjoying sex. So it will come as no surprise when I say tension orgasms are the most common for the largest number of people. While there is no such thing as having the "wrong" kind of orgasm, some are definitely better than others. When a person spends more time building up sexual arousal by breathing, moving, and allowing the body to express a little joy with sounds of pleasure, it will create a more joyful and satisfying experience with orgasm. Fast sex is like fast food—it takes the edge off hunger but it's not all that nourishing.

Relaxation orgasms are difficult to achieve alone because it's nearly impossible to be totally relaxed while doing some form of self-stimulation. My relaxed orgasms first happened in my teens with manual sex from a boyfriend's delicate touch. During long sessions of kissing, I was the classic Sleeping Beauty. To avoid exhibiting any animal-like behavior, I kept releasing the build up of sexual tension by repeatedly relaxing all my muscles. This took major concentration, but I felt my reputation was at stake. At some point, when I could hold back no longer, the orgasm would come and get me. As long as I did nothing to make my orgasm happen and he didn't "put it in," I was still considered a virgin.

The best way to experience a relaxation orgasm is to do it with a partner. Some teachers of Eastern sex techniques have their students take turns giving and receiving manual sex with explicit verbal guidance telling each other exactly when and how to vary the stimulation. They are also taught to slow down, relax the pelvic floor muscles, and breathe to allow the orgasm to build more gradually. Rajneesh, a Tantra teacher from India, called this kind of climax a "valley orgasm"—sinking down into the sensation instead of building up as in a "peak orgasm," which is what I call a tension orgasm.

Rajneesh told his students that people would have a different view of sex in the future; he believed sex would involve more fun, more joy, more friendship, and more play than the serious affair it is now. I wholeheartedly support this image and have incorporated it into my own approach to teaching sex. Two of my heroes, Rajneesh and Wilhelm Reich, both ended up in jail—an indication of how new ideas about sexuality threaten insecure American men and women in government.

Combination orgasms are my favorite, so here is my bias. These orgasms use both tension and relaxation as well as some form of *direct* clitoral stimulation with either fingers or a vibrator, along with vaginal penetration. The combination orgasm is the one I ended up teaching in my masturbation workshops. After a few groups, I realized I could jump-start sexual arousal for women who had never had an orgasm by using the electric vibrator. So I began teaching women how to harness all that power for pleasure. Even women who were already orgasmic with their hands could take their orgasms to the next level by plugging in and masturbating much longer than the usual few minutes. The key to enjoying an electric vibrator is to layer a washcloth over the clitoris to control the intensity of the vibrations. As stimulation continues, a layer is removed.

After getting in touch with our pelvic floor muscle, we did slow penetration with a dildo while squeezing and releasing the PC muscle. Then we added clitoral stimulation with a vibrator. While the hips rock forward and back, the muscles in the body flex and relax similar to those of an athlete in motion. We continued doing slow rhythmic pelvic thrusting along with deep breathing and sounds of pleasure. Just in front of an orgasm, some women's pelvic movements got more urgent, while others slowed down and a few stopped just before climax.

Combining these five elements—clitoral stimulation, vaginal stimulation, PC muscle contractions, pelvic thrusting, and breathing out loud—make the combination orgasm the one that translates the most easily into partnersex. During intercourse, the woman or her partner simply adds her preferred kind of clitoral contact.

Multiple orgasms started getting press after Masters and Johnson documented women having this sexual response. When I first read about multiple orgasms I felt envious, like a lot of other women did. I thought they happened one right after another like a string of pearls breaking—pop, pop, pop. Most of us are grateful to have one orgasm during partnersex, let alone many. I had no idea it was possible to have more than one orgasm until I was thirty-five. One memorable night Grant kept stimulating my clitoris after I came and I ended up having two more giant orgasms before collapsing in a blissful heap, satisfied beyond my wildest dreams.

Later, when I thought about it, I realized that each one of my orgasms had required some kind of build up. During masturbation, moments after having a nice big come, my clitoris was always hypersensitive, so I stopped touching myself. After having that first experience of several orgasms, I softened my clitoral stimulation, stayed with it, and moved into another buildup. From there I could go on to enjoy several more orgasms. Then I discovered the same was true for other women as well; they, too, needed some additional build up to come again. Once I started calling them "serial orgasms," instead of "multiple orgasms," more women could identify with the image and another sexual myth was cleared up.

When women talk about having thirty to forty orgasms in succession, I suspect they are counting the aftershocks of pleasure that follow a big orgasm. These autonomic reflexes can go on for several minutes or longer if we continue clitoral stimulation. While it feels great, I believe the sexual energy is being dissipated from the first full orgasm or two, not thirty new individual orgasms. Because so many men get their self-esteem by taking credit for a woman's sexual response, every twitch or jerk of her body is counted as another orgasm. Women play into this notion, maintaining the idea that multiple orgasms come one right after another. Due to the confusion and misinformation about female sexuality, I'm sure some women are convinced they are telling the truth when they report these large numbers of orgasms.

G-spot orgasms entered the picture in 1982 with the book by the same name, and we were thrown back to the old debate of vaginal vs. clitoral orgasms. The authors claimed that women had a sensitive spot on the ceiling of the vagina. Finding this spot and stimulating it vigorously with a finger could lead to orgasm. An enhancement to the theory was that some of these orgasms are accompanied by "female ejaculation." Since I have already made it clear that I support some form of clitoral stimulation for orgasm, I question the trend to glorify G-spot orgasms accompanied by some kind of mysterious fluid as better, deeper, or more satisfying. For a detailed discussion of the finer point of this new Holy Grail of female orgasm, see Chapter 7, "G-Spot or My-Spot."

Fantasy orgasms or "Look Ma, no hands" are those that some women claim to achieve from sexual fantasy alone. They are either the luckiest women in the world or they are "good girl" holdouts grimly determined to never touch themselves "down there." Why else would a woman want to avoid touching her sex organ? Another possibility is that some of these fantasy orgasms are imaginary. I know a mistress who has convinced her rich married lover that listening to him talk dirty not only turns her on but also gives her passionate orgasms. However, a few white lies are understandable if an important source of your livelihood depends on persuading a man he's the hottest fuck in town.

Every time I hear someone say "The biggest sex organ is between our ears," I agree and I also disagree. While I adore searching my mind for forbidden images that create more arousal, I'll admit I'm attached to playing with the incredible sex organ that's between my legs. Sexual fantasy can definitely enhance orgasm, but emphasizing all that is born of the mind is based on our society's fear and trembling over those unruly sensations and filthy physical functions that emanate from the human body.

The one-hour orgasm is the epitome of sexual hype. There have been articles, books, and videos about women having "one-hour orgasms." This is a man's fantasy of a woman's sexual response. We can enjoy high states of sexual arousal for an hour, and have a series of orgasms over a period of many hours, but no *one* orgasm lasts an hour. In one video, a man does genital massage to a woman who is carrying on sufficiently to win the Academy Award for best actress. Like I said, every twitch or sound a woman makes is proof enough for a power-driven man to be convinced he's making his woman come, and come, and come. She goes along with him to keep the peace or maintain her standard of living—or she also believes she's having a one-hour orgasm.

The meltdown orgasm is a variation on the relaxation orgasm with penetration and clitoral stimulation. It first appeared when Eric and I got together. With a vibrator held near my clitoris, it feels as though the soft spongy tip of his penis is either moving past the mouth of my uterus or gently pressing against the tip of my uterus with slow, deep penetration. Instead of squeezing my PC muscles, I keep everything relaxed. With each deep thrust of his penis, I reach a point where I feel as though my orgasm is building of its own accord, and I know my body will be overtaken by an orgasmic wave. The orgasm is very full and satisfying, but then, I've never had an orgasm I didn't like. Some are just better than others.

The first time I experienced the meltdown orgasm I couldn't wait to do it again. The next time we had sex; those sensations were nowhere to be found. And I knew why. My mind was focusing on any sign of "impending ecstasy." It's similar to wanting simultaneous orgasms—it's very nice when it happens, but if I look for it, expect it, or try to achieve it, I've lost it altogether. Sexual activity continues to be one of my best teachers. I cannot command my body to go into orgasmic ecstasy. I must trust my body, stop thinking, and allow my senses to take over. The minute I think I'm taking too long, or think he's getting close to coming, or wondering if I'm about to catch the orgasmic wave, I'm outside my body looking in. I need to be inside my body focused on the pleasurable sensations.

THE AUTONOMIC NERVOUS SYSTEM

This is the key to having orgasms. Along with all the romantic or commercial versions of female orgasm, I agree with Wilhelm Reich's theory of the two phases of the voluntary and the involuntary control of orgasm. The orgasm reflex is part of the autonomic system. We can consciously control how we are building up sexual excitation, but we are not in control of the actual orgasm.

The autonomic system operates the motor functions of all the internal organs and the smooth muscles in the intestines, blood and lymph vessels, and glands. I can't will my body to come, just as I can't make a decision to sneeze. But I can tickle my clitoris or my nose until my body responds with an orgasm or a sneeze, which are both autonomic reflexes.

In many of my Bodysex groups, we did a position I called the goddess pose, which stretched the inner thigh muscles while opening the pelvic floor. Putting the soles of our feet together and drawing them close to our bodies, we let our legs drop open. After breathing and relaxing the leg muscles while in this position for at least three to five minutes, we very slowly drew up our legs an inch at a time. Everyone's legs would tremble to different degrees as the tension was released. This was an exercise in learning to trust our bodies instead of always trying to control them with our minds. The automatic leg trembling was a demonstration of the autonomic nervous system, which is where our orgasms come from.

There are many forms of sexual stimulation. To one woman it's a tongue on her clitoris; another wants deep vaginal thrusting that pushes against her uterus; still another prefers fingers inside her vagina because her partner has more control; and many want a vibrator on the clitoris alone while others want to combine a vibrator with vaginal penetration. Some sexually advanced women want anal and vaginal penetration along with a vibrator for clitoral stimulation all at once. A few women squirt a small amount of fluid when they come, a few can have orgasms with breast stimulation, and a person with a spinal cord injury can develop a new place to trigger orgasm.

Some women like role-playing and erotic restraints and some want a little light spanking before or during partnersex. Oh, I almost forgot the Tickle Orgasm. We all know that people who are ticklish have probably been conditioned to respond that way by a parent who went tickle, tickle, tickle when they were babies. Several men and women have told me how their lovers have used restraints or tied them to the bed so they were helpless. They were tickled until they were limp from laughter. Then with just a few strokes with a hand on his dick or a feather on her clit, it triggered a big O. Exhaustion equals surrender equals orgasm.

I'm sure I've left out a thousand other ways women as well as men are enjoying their orgasms alone and with their partners. However, I'm positive about one thing: Among all this sexual variety, once a woman discovers what turns her on and is able to clearly state her pleasure, instead of the question "Did you come?" her lover or husband will be asking "Do you want to come again, honey?"

❧ 7 ❧

G-SPOT OR MY-SPOT
Reaffirming the Clitoris

A LOT OF WEIRD THINGS HAPPENED in the early eighties that ended a good part of the sexual freedom many of us had enjoyed during the seventies. There are still theories circulating as to what took place to curtail our sexual liberties. Some say it was the AIDS virus spreading among the gay men's community that made sex equal death. Others claim it was heterosexual men's backlash from too much sexual freedom for women. Many feminist spokeswomen complained that the sexual revolution was for the benefit of men only. When Women Against Pornography was formed some feminists took a wrong turn by supporting this well-funded organization, which revived the call for censorship of sexual images. All in all I felt caught in the middle of a sexual disaster that seemed to be masterminded by some secret government agency—maybe the CIA.

As if that wasn't bad enough, *The G-Spot* by Alice Kahn Ladas, Beverly Whipple, and Dr. John D. Perry came out in 1982, herald-ing the return of a new kind of vaginal orgasm, one where women ejaculated. The book was full of glorious testimonials giving ejac-ulating orgasms rave reviews. Their theory claimed the G-spot freed us from thinking of vaginal vs. clitoral orgasm. Just as there are two ways for men to climax—from the penis and the prostate gland—the same was true for women. We could climax from our clits or our G-spots. They pointed out that while it was easy for a woman to touch her clitoris, she needed a partner to stimulate her G-spot. The same thing was true for a man. It was easy enough for a man to simulate his penis, but he needed a partner to reach his prostate. Evidently they were not aware that either a woman or man could do themselves with a dildo.

The timing of the book was perfect. As couples headed back into a more strict monogamy to avoid death from casual sex, they had a new game to play. They could look for each other's spots—hers inside the vagina and his inside the rectum. Just when I thought the clitoris had been reinstated, men and women started digging around inside vaginas searching for some magic spot.

The four basic ideas presented in *The G-Spot* was information that had been published before and then forgotten. The first was the Grafenberg spot, the second was female ejaculation, the third was the importance of pelvic muscle tone, and the fourth was the continuum of orgasmic response. I was all for pelvic muscle tone and the various orgasmic responses, but erotic spots inside the vagina didn't make sense to me. There was a reason the clitoris with its eight thousand nerve endings was above the birth canal, and the idea of women ejaculating like men was weird.

Next I read that every woman had a G-spot, but not all of us would respond to its being stimulated. Well, if I had one, why couldn't I respond? The authors said it might be because my PC muscle was weak or chronically tense. Or wearing a diaphragm all those years had covered "my spot." Maybe I had retrograde ejaculations and peed them out later, or I had repressed my ejaculations, thinking it was urine. Finally, it could also be the result of menopause; "my spot" had dried up from lack of hormones. Reading all those glowing accounts from women and men who carried on and on about these ecstatic gushing rushing orgasms from vaginal stimulation made me and a lot of other women feel like inadequate clit nerds.

On one of my trips to San Francisco to run a workshop, I asked my friend Carol Queen what she thought about G-spots and female ejaculation. At the time she was working at the sex store GoodVibrations. She said she was learning how to do it along with several other women. When I asked exactly what she was doing, she said she was using vaginal stimulation with a dildo while holding a vibrator on her clit. Right before she came, she'd pull the dildo out and bear down with her PC muscle to squirt. Since these women were much younger, I made an effort to withhold judgment. After all, I was a postmenopausal woman in my fifties, and might be getting a bit set in my ways.

During that same trip, I went to an evening presentation of several erotic videos produced by lesbians. One of the videos, *Clips,* showed a bored housewife who couldn't interest her husband in having sex, so she started fucking herself with a dildo. It took me several minutes before I realized the guy sitting in the corner of the room reading a newspaper was a woman in male drag. After some very "vigorous thrusting," the wife removed the dildo and shot a stream from her pussy with the force of a fire hose. I absolutely adored the video and roared with laughter, but I didn't for one minute believe she was having an authentic orgasm. For me, the whole video was a fabulous spoof on butch/femme roles and heterosexuality.

The woman turned out to be Fannie Fatale, who would later make the video *How to Female Ejaculate.* Fannie obviously has a strong PC muscle, which I could relate to. I used to have a douching technique where I'd fill up my vagina with water and then

force it out. The stream of water went the length of my big bathtub, hitting the faucet three feet away. I figured she either filled up
her vagina with water and then they cut to her orgasm sequence,
or she drank a lot of water beforehand and peed. When my friends
insisted she was ejaculating, I concluded that whatever rocks a gal's
fantasy boat is fine with me. As far as I was concerned, female ejaculation was just a new twist on the old "golden showers" routine
of urinating for fun. I was clearly out of step with most of the lesbian and bisexual San Francisco women on this one.

Back in the fifties, before lesbian feminists classified butch/
femme roles as politically incorrect, my best girlfriend was a lipstick lesbian. We both loved drawing nudes, so we shared the cost
of a model once a week in my art studio. One day Lois told me
she'd learned to pee right after she had an orgasm so her butch
lover, Fran, would know for sure when she came. I thought it was
very considerate of her and asked how she did it. Lois liked having
sex with a full bladder because it gave her more sensation during
oral sex and finger fucking. Immediately after her orgasm, she'd
bear down and force urine out. Today I'd call that fantasy role-
playing rather than female ejaculation.

On each of my West Coast trips, I kept posing questions about
female ejaculation to my women friends who were sexually knowledgeable. At one point Carol Queen and her partner, Robert

---

*Here we see a frontal view showing the erectile tissue of the female genitals.
The glands of the clitoris have approximately eight thousand nerve endings.
The shaft and legs (or crus) are long, thin bands of firm tissue that fill
with blood during sexual arousal. The legs of the clitoris flare outward along
the pubic bone. The bulb of the clitoris is a spongy body made up of a
more elastic tissue that also becomes erect and lies underneath the outer lips.
Another spongy body surrounds the urinary tract. Since this structure
was not named in textbooks, feminists named it the urethral sponge. The
vulvovaginal, or Bartholin, glands on either side of the vaginal opening
secrete a few drops of fluid during sexual arousal.*

The pelvic bone showing the position of the genitals.

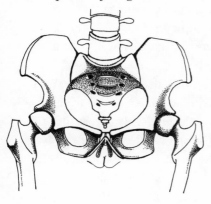

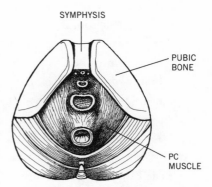

The important PC, or pubococcygeus, muscle circles the anus, vagina, urethra, and clitoris and attaches to the pubic bone. It determines the health and pleasure of men and women's sexual function.

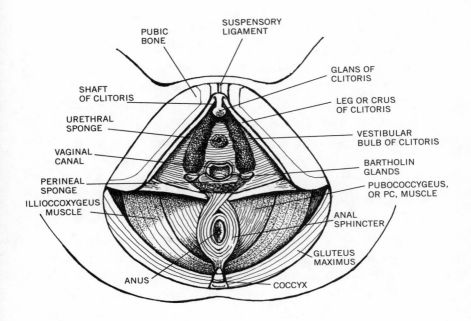

The Internal Structure of the Female Genitals

Lawrence, asked if I wanted to dissect the female genitals on a cadaver at a school in Oakland? Without any hesitation I said yes. After making the arrangements, the three of us took off on a sunny afternoon for our adventure. Standing in a large room with cadavers lying around in black bags wasn't upsetting to me. After all, I'd been an art student who had drawn the nude as well as studied anatomy books. I felt right at home.

As we all watched intently, Helen, our anatomist with twenty years' experience, slowly removed thin layers of tissue from the female cadaver's genitals. Finally, she uncovered a gland that she said looked just like a male prostate, only much smaller. What I saw was a green pickled lump that could have been anything. She said this was the first time she'd ever dissected the female genitals—the most fascinating information of the entire experiment. Otherwise our dissection only raised more questions.

Along with the authors of *The G-Spot,* I agree that men and women have more in common than is usually acknowledged. After going through several anatomy books, I saw for myself that the male prostate originated in the undifferentiated female embryo. The prostate gland in men secretes an alkaline fluid that is discharged with the sperm to keep them healthy. I could see how a small amount of the same alkaline fluid could be discharged by a woman's paraurethral gland.

The first person to describe the female prostate in detail was seventeenth-century Dutch anatomist Reinier de Graaf, who also considered its erotic aspects. In the late 1800s, Dr. Alexander Skene was only concerned with draining the various glands surrounding the female urethra when it became infected. To this day the female urethral glands are known as Skene's glands. In 1950, Dr. Ernst Grafenberg (the "G" in the G-spot) noted that some women emitted fluid during orgasm, and he believed it came from the urethral glands. The authors of *The G-Spot* didn't mention the Bartholin's glands, which are the size of two lima beans on either side of the vaginal opening.

The feminist self-helpers who wrote *A New View of a Woman's Body*, which came out in 1981, called the Bartholin's glands the vulvovaginal glands. They said they didn't seem to have any function other than to secrete a few drops of fluid during sexual arousal. They also called the spongy tissue surrounding the female urinary tract the urethral sponge; it had a network of tiny ducts inside called the paraurethral gland. The plot thickens and gets more confusing as different researchers give different names to the same parts of the internal female genitals.

By the nineties, G-spot orgasms were all the rage in San Francisco. One young lesbian, who identified herself as a "sex educator," wrote an article in the GoodVibrations newsletter announcing, "Now that we've rediscovered the G-spot, vaginal orgasms are back in style!" She also proudly claimed that many dykes had been at the forefront in the movement to reclaim the G-spot. She even went so far as to describe female ejaculation as "spewing forth buckets of liquid"—mindlessly creating another sexual myth and making nonejaculating women feel less than sexual.

Female ejaculation should more accurately be called female fluid emission. Yes, I believe there are some women who naturally have this response. With each contraction of the pelvic floor muscles, a fine spray comes out of the urethral opening without any effort or consciously bearing down. Female fluid emission has been written about throughout history. However, as in most erotic literature or personal testimony, sex gets described in exaggerated and glowing terms. It's called poetic license. Added to that is the idea that during the last two decades, goddess forbid any person, especially a woman, ever doubted another woman's anecdotal testimony. If you did, you were considered antifeminist or antiwoman.

The pendulum always swings too far in both directions. For example, as a result of finally dealing with the sexual abuse of women, we went completely overboard. An abuse industry grew up around women's accusations of being raped, encouraged by therapists who were later discovered to be creating false memories in their clients. I believe this is similar to the creation of a G-spot industry. We now have G-spot toys as well as other books and videos on the subject. So what's in a name? Everything, when we turn it into the latest sexual fashion, confusing people even further about female orgasm.

Most people assume the word "ejaculation" equals or accompanies sexual arousal and orgasm, which is not true for all women who have this response. Many of my women friends who are performance artists admit their ability to "shoot liquid" has nothing to do with being sexually turned on, nor is it the result of having an orgasm. They are doing it because it feels great, it's fun, and it has a lot of entertainment value.

At one of Annie Sprinkle's photo shoots I watched Shannon Bell kneel, put her finger inside her vagina, and rapidly move it in and out for a few moments. Then she pushed down to squirt. She did this several times while Annie clicked away. During a break, while Shannon was drinking a beer, I asked if she was having sexual sensations during her multiple ejaculations? She very candidly

---

FIGURE A *shows the clitoris, the urethral sponge, and the vagina, which is a collapsed space until it is penetrated. The urethral sponge fills with blood during sexual excitement and protects the urinary tract from friction caused by the penis moving back and forth inside the vagina during intercourse.*

In FIGURE B *we see a finger entering the vagina and pressing up into the urethral sponge, or what has been called the "G-spot." This spongy area is more like a crest than a specific spot. Some women find this kind of pressure on the vaginal ceiling to be sexually arousing but many others do not.*

In FIGURE C *we see the paraurethral gland inside the urethra without the surrounding sponge. These glands in the female remain the size of those of a five-month-old male fetus but they go on to develop into the much larger prostate gland in the male. Some believe these the paraurethral glands in women are the source of female fluid emission. We also see the position of the tiny openings of Skene's glands.*

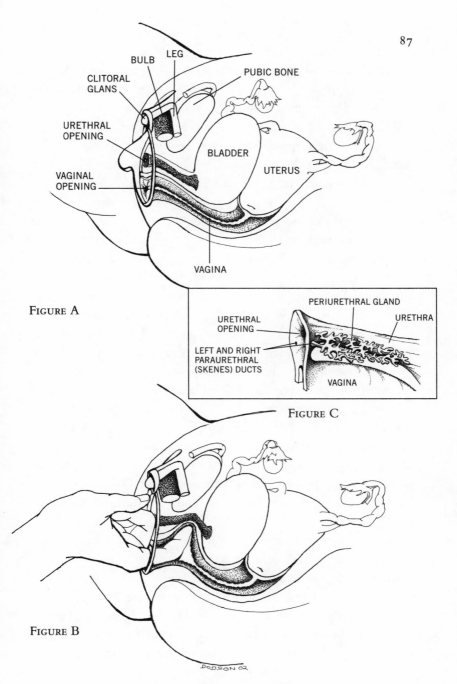

Side View of the Female Genitals

said no, she was just doing it for the camera. Shannon is an adorable
little androgynous dyke who is a very intelligent writer. She was in
the video *How to Female Ejaculate* that starred Fannie Fatale, along
with Carol Queen and Baja, a woman I never met.

Carol is a performance artist who has since become a noted
author and a Ph.D. sex educator. During another one of our many
ongoing sex conversations, I again asked how she thought all of that
liquid could come out of the little bit of spongy tissue or female
prostate gland that we had uncovered. She speculated that after a
couple of spurts, she was probably borrowing urine from her bladder. She said, "So what? It still feels great." At last, I'd heard a statement from a woman ejaculator that I believed. Due to our puritan
heritage and religious disgust over all bodily fluids, peeing for fun
is not acceptable, but "ejaculation" sounds sexy, so it's okay.

At one of her stage performances, my friend and former neighbor Annie Sprinkle sailed by a group of us waiting in line to see
her show. Smiling, she held up a large bottle of water and said,
"Guess what I'm doing tonight?" When Annie was a porn star I
believe she picked the stage name Sprinkle for golden showers,
which is still a favorite sexual image of many men. Annie has
become a sexual icon who has expanded people's ideas about porn
stars and whores as victims by becoming a successful photographer,
writer, and performance artist. She now has her Ph.D. in sexology
from the Institute for the Advanced Study of Human Sexuality in
San Francisco.

Kim Airs, another friend, owns a sex store in Boston called
Grand Opening! She's very intelligent as well as a good business-
woman. Similar to Annie, her brilliance is putting people at ease by
getting them to laugh about sex. Kim runs ongoing events and
workshops. My favorite workshop is "How to Strip," but I com-
plain about her teaching female ejaculation. Kim has a marvelous
sense of humor. She can squirt anywhere, anytime, and loves doing
it. While I badger her about peeing on my rug, she laughs and tells
me I'm jealous. She says her ejaculate doesn't taste or smell like

urine. That's when I ask who's her expert on how urine tastes and why does it matter? If I'm proved wrong, I promised her she can drench me with her love juice from head to clit.

These ongoing dialogues with my women friends, who are mostly bisexual and enjoying active sex lives, are always informative. They are in the sex business because they like sex. They all know I question the feasibility of teaching a woman to squirt while she has a sexual climax. Sometimes we end up agreeing to disagree.

My current understanding is that the orgasm reflex is part of the autonomic nervous system that cannot be controlled by the mind. Consciously bearing down to emit fluid would require the mind to dominate the body. Theoretically, one could have an orgasm and *then* make an effort to emit fluid. But bearing down right before orgasm would be like blowing your nose in front of a sneeze—it would short-circuit the autonomic reflex. Another possibility is that strong vaginal finger or dildo friction acts like a catheter and causes the bladder to empty right before orgasm. While that might feel great, I don't believe wet orgasms are more desirable than old-fashioned dry ones.

Teachers of female ejaculation completely contradict the description of how to do Kegel exercises to strengthen the pelvic floor muscle. They are telling their students to bear down or push out during masturbation or intercourse. This is not the best use of the pelvic floor muscles. Women who consciously bear down as they would during childbirth when they want to have an orgasm appear to be losing the lining of their vaginas, with the uterus about to follow. Those bulging vaginal vestibules do not indicate strong pelvic floor muscles, rather the reverse. How do I know this? I've sat alongside thousands of women looking into the same mirror while we view their genitals together. Maybe I'll end up in the *Guinness Book of Records* for having seen the largest number of women's genitals up close and personal.

One of my clients, a postmenopausal woman, said she and her boyfriend had learned about the G-spot in a Tantra workshop. They called it the sacred spot. Although Louise wasn't sure if she'd ever had an orgasm, she did learn to "ejaculate." To get her lover to stop rubbing inside her vagina when it became painful, she arched her back and shot out a stream of pee, accompanied by a bloodcurdling scream. Although he was thrilled, she kept feeling there must be more to orgasm and came to see me. We discovered her PC muscle was very weak. It will take a few months of practice to retrain her pelvic floor muscles to lift up during sexual arousal. She left with an electric vibrator, Betty's Barbell, and my directions on doing clitoral stimulation while practicing her Kegels so it will be pleasurable and motivate her to do it more frequently.

The idea of coming from vaginal stimulation is still one of America's number one fetishes, and now we can add drenching the sheets as number two. Women's magazines continue to publish articles about female ejaculation, and the same information is automatically included in every new book about sex. The Internet is full of home and adult videos showing women shooting out big streams of fluid, claiming it is female ejaculation. Many women insist these new wet vaginal orgasms are the cat's meow. Questions from women and men visiting my website continue to ask how to find the G-spot, but occasionally a woman wants to stop lying in a wet puddle.

One twenty-year-old woman said that when she is using a vibrator on her clitoris, still warming up and feeling pretty good, she loses control of her bladder and pees. A few minutes later she'll have an orgasm. She doesn't mind this too much, since her orgasms are well worth it, but what happens when she's with a lover? How does she go about alleviating this problem? My answer is for her to observe how she is using her pelvic floor muscles. She needs to start using my Barbell and doing her Kegel exercises to strengthen her PC muscle or learn to relax the muscle if it's chronically contracted.

Several other friends contradict the idea of stimulating the G-spot to squirt. One younger woman learned how to ejaculate by watching the video, but she only does clitoral stimulation manually. She says ejaculating feels similar to having a good cry. One older friend has spewed only three times in her life, with a vibrator on her clitoris, but she remains enamored of an eleven-inch wet spot left on her bed years ago. She steadfastly insists it was not urine. I tease her, asking if women will end up measuring their degree of pleasure relative to the size of the wet spot left on the bed?

In the mid-nineties, Gary Schubach was at my house one night and we got into discussing whether the fluid was prostatic in nature or urine. He was dedicated to the idea of the new erotic possibilities for manual stimulation and offered to demonstrate G-spot stimulation with his girlfriend. As I observed, he used a rapid finger friction inside her vagina while she appeared to be giving birth by bearing down. My objection was that it seemed to me to be more performance-oriented than pleasure-based.

A couple of years later, in 1997, Gary did an experiment as part of his Ph.D. thesis to determine whether female ejaculation came from the urethral sponge or the bladder. He tested seven subjects, who were all female ejaculators. Urine specimens were collected from each woman before she was sexually aroused. They used self-stimulation of the vagina with their fingers or a curved dildo or finger penetration by a partner. The clitoris was never mentioned. After an hour, when the subjects felt ready to ejaculate, a catheter was inserted. Their bladders were drained and the collection bag changed. Then they all had what each woman and the medical team considered to be an ejaculatory orgasm.

The conclusion from the experiment was that the vast majority of the fluid came from their bladders. Even though their bladders had been drained before ejaculation, they still expelled from 50 to 900 milliliters of fluid. The liquid was a combination of fluid from the walls of the bladder and from new kidney output. The clear inference was that the expelled fluid was an altered form of urine with a reduced concentration of urea and creatinine.

Over the years, whenever I'd see Beverly Whipple at a sex conference, I'd say, "I can't find my G-spot but I'm still looking." She would laugh and then shake her head in exasperation. She's a very dedicated woman, and always has a hundred projects going at once. In 1998, Beverly chaired a panel I was on at the Society for the Scientific Study of Sexuality. I began my segment by telling everyone that I finally found my G-spot—it was my urethral sponge or little prostate gland. The floor of my urinary tract was the ceiling of my vagina, and while I enjoyed some pressure there with a finger, dildo, or penis, I'd never "ejaculated." My-Spot was the combination of clitoral and vaginal stimulation at the same time, which gave me great orgasms. Best of all, I could do it all by myself.

In 2001 another friend and sex therapist, Dr. Joanna Whitcup, forwarded an e-mail exchange between several members of the Female Sexual Function Forum (FSFF). They were discussing a case where clitoral stimulation induced urination. Dr. John Perry, one of the authors of *The G-Spot,* pointed out that the current hot topic in female ejaculation is whether large-volume expulsions of fluid, usually considered to be, or examined and determined to be, dilute urine, should be included as a normal variant of female ejaculation. According to all the reports, women who learn how to do this insist that it feels wonderful. Perry said the original *G-Spot* authors insist that only the output of the female paraurethral glands (prostate equivalent) should be considered female ejaculation, and that's never more than a couple of teaspoonfuls at most.

There remains an enormous amount of confusion when it comes to female sexual response, even for me. While some women emit a small amount of fluid with orgasm, the vast majority of us do not. Personally, I have no problem adding urination orgasms to my long list of things that feel good. I'm not against anyone doing anything that turns women on as long as it doesn't harm anyone and it's consensual. Currently, my best orgasm comes from direct clitoral stimulation along with penetration. But no one orgasm stands alone as the pinnacle of female sexual response for all of womankind. Pleasure rules.

❧ 8 ❧

MASTURBATION FOR COUPLES
Sexual Compatibility

O NE OF THE BEST FOUNDATIONS for building and sustaining sexual compatibility and mutual orgasms is based upon each person's acceptance of masturbation. In a sex-positive society both partners would start off with some degree of sex for one skill before attempting sex for two. Once they establish a committed partnership, they understand that masturbation will be an ongoing process throughout their lives together. They know that self-sexuality is a way for each of them to privately explore their erotic minds through sexual fantasies. They both agree that sharing masturbation in each other's presence is the cornerstone for creating an even deeper level of sexual intimacy.

While this might sound like a futuristic scenario for the year 3000, sophisticated couples of all sexual orientations are living this way today, including myself. Due to the restrictions of censorship, this more liberated view of partnersex never sees the light of day. Instead, we are shown a sexual conformity of Mr. and Mrs. Normal who are happily married, sexually compatible, monogamous, raising at least one child, and remain together throughout a lifetime. This is only true for a very small minority, so we need to cut the majority of us a little slack. We are all entitled to be sexually fulfilled.

Change is inevitable; it is a natural part of the human condition. More than half the population will have several marriages. For many, sexual variety remains the spice of life, and they like being single. There are people who choose to be celibate; others prefer self-sexuality. I know an older couple who say they still enjoy partnersex after forty-some years of marriage, and they have never included masturbation. So even the inclusion of masturbation for every couple to be happy is not etched in stone.

At the beginning of my first postmarital relationship, with Grant, I decided not to lie about my adult masturbation anymore. I spoke openly about how masturbation had kept me sane during marriage. He admitted masturbation filled in for him, too. Gradually we started telling each other about our different experiences with masturbation. This required trust. I had to trust that the person I claimed to love could handle the truth about my masturbation history, which centered around clitoral stimulation. That put an end to the idea that I'd ever been able to successfully transfer my sexual pleasure from my clitoris to my vagina—so much for coming from Romeo's penis.

SHARING MASTURBATION HISTORIES

My first memory was riding in the backseat of the family car when I was five years old. Daddy had started a new job in California and we were joining him there. Adventure was in the air. While Mother chatted with my older brother in the front seat, my two younger brothers were asleep next to me on a pile of blankets in the backseat. At that moment I must have felt that it was safe enough to pull a pillow up between my legs and rock back and forth on it until "the tickle" went away.

In my forties, while writing my first article about masturbation, I called Mother to confirm this memory. Yes, she remembered the incident clearly, because she had seen me in the rearview mirror. She said that wasn't the first or last time she'd seen me with a pillow between my legs. I told her I still slept with a pillow between my legs, but now when I masturbated I used a vibrator. Not long after that conversation, I sent Mother a Magic Wand to soothe her sore muscles. She later told me that the machine I gave her was absolutely marvelous for "You know what."

Today I believe my happy childhood masturbation shaped aspects of my life. First, I was not punished for the innocent act of self-pleasuring. Maybe having my first memory anchored in the security of my family explains why I was able to exhibit drawings of people masturbating, teach masturbation in workshops, and write several books devoted to this otherwise taboo subject. For me, self-stimulation was a natural act until I learned differently once the social conditioning of school began.

Our sexual beginnings give us valuable insights into ourselves as well as one another. It's very informative when couples can talk about their first memories of masturbation, the kind of technique they used, and what it felt like. Grant doesn't have a first memory of masturbation. He remembered his dick getting hard and rubbing it felt really nice. However, his first orgasm at thirteen is clear as a bell, with precise recall on the room, the furniture, time of day, and how it felt when he shot his first ejaculate. I, on the other hand, have no memory of my first orgasm. For me it was a tickle that went away until the sensation gradually grew more intense.

Getting caught in the act of playing with our sex organs by a parent or a sibling can be traumatic. Children who are severely controlled, punished, scolded, or humiliated can develop sexual problems that last a lifetime. One girlfriend grew up with a serious masturbation taboo. When her mother tucked her into bed at night as a toddler, she slipped the cardboard rolls from toilet paper over her daughter's little hands so she wouldn't touch herself "down there." For her, even saying the word "masturbation" out loud was difficult. She was able to masturbate when she and her husband were apart, but she was never able to share masturbation in his presence. After hearing her gruesome history, he understood.

Another friend had a nanny who placed the rubber sheet that protected the mattress over his little penis and rubbed it—an acceptable activity to calm a crying child in some cultures. As an adult, touching or wearing rubber gives him a strong erotic charge. Fortunately these days, fashion has normalized the wearing of many fetish-type clothes, such as leather and clothes made out of high-quality latex. Another girlfriend remembers going into her parent's bedroom whenever they were not at home and masturbating while wearing one of her mom's silk slips. To this day wearing silk arouses her.

MARITAL MASTURBATION

Of the many couples who have shared the truth with me about their sex lives, the ones that are the most comfortable with monogamy usually enjoy masturbation for sexual variety. Even those couples that share sex with other people either openly or surreptitiously agree on the important role that sex with oneself plays in keeping sexual interests healthy in a primary relationship. Connoisseurs of the erotic know the importance of continuing to have sex with themselves, while the sexually traditional think there will be no need for solo sex once they have a partner.

During a conversation I had with Mr. Macho, who had already gone through three wives at forty, he made it abundantly clear that he never had to masturbate. Yet he also claimed he was faithful to every woman he loved. When I asked what he'd do if he was separated from his current girlfriend for a month, he said he'd just get a blowjob and remain monogamous. For him, having to do himself was a sign of weakness or sexual failure. There will always be those men who believe that once they are in a committed relationship or married, masturbation will not figure into their lives anymore.

Having sex with oneself within a committed partnership solves a myriad of problems such as temporary periods of separation, having a baby, health issues, and work-related travel. For a multitude of reasons, our patterns of desire also differ greatly. No two people will consistently want sex at the same time and with the same frequency year in and year out. A woman may enjoy sex twice a week while her husband wants sex every day. She might make an effort to accommodate him at first, but in time resentments will grow. If he's free to masturbate on the five days she's not interested, they will both enjoy sex more equally when they do get together. The reverse could also be true. She wants sex more frequently than he. Masturbation allows each partner to satisfy his or her own individual sexual needs and appetites.

The year Eric and I began living together, we had sex nearly every day. By the second year, I was happy with partnersex once or twice a week. He still wanted one or two orgasms a day. At night he sometimes watches porn in his room doing some Jo, or jacking off. (For women, Jo means jilling off.) During the day, he likes to masturbate sitting on the bathroom floor—a habit he developed at college, where the bathroom was the only place for privacy. Since he's been living with me he rarely closes the door. Every time I happen to walk past the bathroom and see him sitting on the floor intently playing with his peter, my heart swells with unconditional love. Once again I'm filled with gratitude for a partnership that is based on the complete acceptance of masturbation without any reservations from either of us. It offers us both a great deal of sexual freedom and comfort.

Over the years, I've had women tell me that when they discover their husband masturbates they think something is being taken away from them, or they feel like sexual failures. If they discover he's watching X-rated videos, looking at pictures of naked women online, or going to chat rooms while he masturbates, many spiral into a jealous rage. This hard-line definition of sexual fidelity destroys any chance of a man's enjoying a little harmless sexual variety through masturbation and fantasy. The same is true of men who feel threatened when they discover their wives are enjoying orgasms by masturbating with a vibrator.

This kind of possessiveness is based upon a great deal of sexual insecurity. Do we really feel so sexually inadequate that when our partner has a few private moments of erotic pleasure alone we believe the worst—they are on their way out the door to dump us for someone who is better at sex?

Sex with oneself tends to be easier than partnersex when it comes to having an orgasm, a fact few of us want to acknowledge. Not all couples desire penetration sex all the time. She might have her period. He might be tired and prefer masturbation to intercourse for an easy climax. Perhaps a recent illness has lowered his or her energy and the idea of making love seems like too much effort.

Far too many men have been brainwashed to believe that fucking is the height of eroticism and masturbation is kid stuff that doesn't count. Not true. Having an orgasm with oneself can often be the most satisfying sex of all. Women know masturbation gives them the most sensation, but then that's not information they want to share for fear of being looked upon as frigid or, more recently, sexually dysfunctional.

COUPLES SHARING MASTURBATION

Revealing our sexual selves in each other's presence will gradually diminish self-consciousness, shame, and embarrassment—three of the biggest barriers to sexual intimacy. When I didn't feel comfortable touching my own genitals in front of my partner, I was full of inhibitions that limited my ability to fully enjoy myself. Coming from the traditional romantic image of being sexually awakened by my prince, what on earth would he think if he saw me whacking off all by myself? That would totally destroy any semblance of romance. Or so I thought.

My sexual healing took place in stages. First, Grant and I admitted we had relied on sneaky guilt-ridden marital masturbation for a good portion of our orgasms. Although we wanted to masturbate together, getting around to actually doing it took several weeks of agreeing that "tonight is the night," but then canceling at the last minute to have intercourse. Before I could get up the courage to share an activity I had kept hidden my entire life, I first had to watch myself masturbating in front of a mirror alone. What did I expect? Maybe I thought I'd look weird, but what I saw was a woman being intense and sexual. As an artist who painted nudes, I saw an image I knew I had to capture at some point.

Once we made this breakthrough, our intimacy deepened. We were able to be more honest about when and how we wanted to share sex together. When I had my period, or his back was bothering him, we could now masturbate together. It greatly lightened our sex life by eliminating the idea that we had to please each other through intercourse all the time. That demand often turns partner-sex into a performance to keep the other person happy.

We also learned how each of us handled our own genitals, and that improved our manual sex technique. During intercourse, if he came before I did, he could now do manual sex for me nearly as well as I did. Or I could do myself while he did a little hot talk. Again the reverse was true. If he needed more direct stimulation to come, he didn't have to fuck faster and harder struggling to get off. I could do him by hand.

It can be very exciting to watch a lover masturbate. Taking turns being a voyeur, watching while your partner is putting on a live sex show, is first-rate titillation. Lying side by side doing it simultaneously, or both of you standing in front of a full-length mirror watching yourself and each other, surpasses most pornography. Sitting in chairs opposite each other in the living room will leave sexual memories lingering in the room. Lying down feet to feet facing each other in bed inspires a little hot talk as you intensify your erotic gaze. One of my favorites is lying side by side with my head opposite the hand that's working his dick for my preference of a close-up. I love to watch a man's dick blow out a load of semen.

Sharing masturbation can be extremely challenging for many women. One example of an inhibited forty-something wife comes from a man who wrote to me saying that both he and his wife masturbate privately. Although she is finally able to talk about it with him, she is not able to masturbate in his presence because of her embarrassment. He wondered if I could offer any help.

I suggested he reach down with well-oiled fingers and massage her clitoris the next time they are having intercourse. After doing this a few times, he can put her hand on her clitoris and encourage her to stimulate herself while he continues to slowly move inside her vagina. Once she is comfortable touching her clitoris during partnersex, it's not such a big leap to masturbate in front of him. Several weeks later he wrote again and thanked me, saying it had worked.

MAINTAINING PRIVATE SOLO SEX IN A PARTNERSHIP

It's important when two people are living together that masturbating separately remain part of each person's sex life. While it's true that masturbating privately will probably not happen during the first months or year, when sex is still new and hot, eventually things will cool down no matter how much we love our partner. Resuming sex with ourselves will benefit the partnership. Those moments of sexual solitude allow us to focus on our own sensations of pleasure without having to be aware of the other person.

In order to grow and develop sexually, this private inner journey is a time to explore our erotic minds in solitude. Some might want to practice masturbation as a sexual meditation to quiet the mind. Those who are learning new skills prefer to practice alone, like a dancer working out at the barre. After all, our partners are an audience of one, so sex for two is similar to a performance. Instead of denigrating the concept of "performing," I say get better at sex and enjoy the applause from an enthusiastic lover.

For those women who are looking for a first orgasm after being in a marriage or a committed relationship for however many years, I recommend they first practice alone. It is essential for a woman to focus entirely on what she is feeling. No matter how well-meaning her partner is, chances are fairly good that he will be a distraction. Women have been caretakers for centuries, so it's difficult for most of us to put ourselves first. The other problem is that men have been programmed to be the provider— of the family's home and hearth and women's sexual pleasure— so it is nearly impossible for them to remain supportive without taking some degree of control. When we are alone, there is always more freedom to concentrate while we are practicing any art form.

One client was in her early seventies when she finally learned how to have an orgasm with an electric vibrator. Following my advice, she and her husband discussed her need to spend time practicing alone. Whenever she closed the bedroom door, he respected her privacy. A year later I got a call from her husband to thank me. He told me how they had incorporated the vibrator into their sex lives. Although she was never able to masturbate in front of him because of her inhibitions, she would masturbate while he sat outside the bedroom door. The sound of the vibrator humming became very arousing and he would also masturbate. When she had her orgasm, she would cry out his name. Whereupon he bounded into the bedroom with a hardon and penetrated her now ready vagina to have his orgasm. They were ecstatic with their new orgasmic sex life.

PARTNER-ASSISTED MASTURBATION

Some of my very best orgasms have been the result of masturbating while a lover does wonderful things to my body. Sometimes it's licking or sucking my nipples; other times it's doing slow in and out penetration with fingers or a dildo. Especially for women with short arms like myself, having a lover work my dildo is highly enjoyable. Or the addition of two extra hands caressing my body all over while I use my vibrator is absolute heaven. The assister gets the visual of his or her partner consumed with the combination of sensations.

On some days when Eric pulls on my robe with his teeth like a little doggie, tugging me toward the bed, he's irresistible. I stop whatever I'm doing and join him. If I'm not in the mood for intercourse, partner-assisted masturbation is always fun. By the time I've reached for the massage oil, he has a hardon. He gets pushed over on his back and I start oiling his cock and balls. While he takes over his penis, I massage and lick his balls or stroke his buttyhole while he masturbates. Being close to the pungent smell of his testicles and watching him shoot a big load gives me more energy than a coffee break.

With my first ongoing woman lover, partner-assisted masturbation helped us through our feelings of tentativeness. We were both new at having sex with women, but we were proficient masturbators. Instead of doing oralsex or strapping on a dildo, which would have been a more advanced form of lesbian sex, we took turns heightening each other's masturbation. During our five-year relationship, Laura and I ended up doing everything. As it turned out, our favorite form of sexual intimacy was sharing hours of massage and masturbation. The nondemanding sensuous touching of massage and being in charge of creating our own orgasms was healing us from years of feeling we had to please our lovers even if it meant sacrificing our own pleasure.

PARTNER-ASSISTED MASTURBATION. *A woman is using her electric vibrator to stimulate her clitoris while her partner heightens her experience of orgasm with some form of erotic vaginal and anal touching or penetration.*

The freedom to satisfy individual sexual desires frees men and women to get closer and be more in touch with each other, literally and figuratively. When it comes to affectionate touching, we can never get enough. One friend wishes her husband gave her half the affection that he lavishes on the dog. Another hesitates to hug her husband for fear he will misconstrue her show of affection as an invitation to have sex. Once couples incorporate masturbation into their partnersex and both know they are free to have an orgasm at any time, displays of affection with touching, hugging, and kissing can take on a life of their own.

THE HISTORY OF MASTURBATION

We would be wise to ask ourselves why people are so terrified of masturbation. When we take into account the entirety of humankind's recorded history, the masturbation taboo is relatively recent. Touching one's own genitals for sexual gratification has been practiced since the Stone Age. Small clay sculptures of masturbating figures dating from that time show acceptance of this human activity. Greek pottery from the fourth and fifth centuries B.C. depicts both women and men joyfully masturbating, along with graphic images of dildo use.

In ancient Egypt, the most popular creation myth was based on a daily masturbation ritual that took place in the Karnak temples built over four thousand years ago—information long-suppressed by scholars and religious authorities due to the embarrassment it still causes. The following text was taken from a wall at Karnak:

> In the beginning there was chaos. Chaos was darkness, the waters
> of the abyss. The first God, Amon, arose from the waters using
> nothing but his own strength to give form to his body. Amon
> existed alone. All was his. Yesterday and tomorrow was his. Alone
> he took his penis in his hand. He made love to his fist. He made
> his exquisite joy with his fingers, and from the flame of the fiery
> blast which he kindled with his hand, the universe was formed.

At dawn every morning, priests and priestesses passed through the processional hallways that linked the three temples, arriving at the last room, the one that held the shrine of Amon Ra. There they reenacted the original creation of divine masturbation to raise the sun god for another glorious day. These ancient Egyptians self-created the source of their own spiritual power on a daily basis with divine masturbation—quite a departure from the majority of religions, which profane the human body and all forms of sexual pleasure.

In ancient Ireland, the Gaelic word for masturbation meant "self-love," but with the arrival of Christianity it was changed overnight into "self-abuse." Religious leaders had successfully turned a natural human activity into a sin for which God would punish them. The biblical story of Onan, who spilled his seed upon

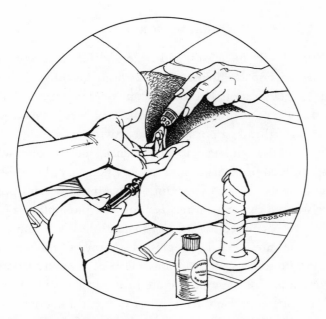

DOUBLE PENETRATION. *Here we see a close-up of simultaneous vaginal and anal penetration while the woman uses a small battery-operated vibrator to stimulate her clitoris. Using plenty of massage oil, her partner heightens her pleasure by penetrating her vagina with his finger and then holding still. He then eases the Barbell inside her anus as she squeezes and releases her PC muscle. Once she is relaxed, he gently and slowly begins moving his finger and the Barbell in a counterpoint rhythm.*

the ground and was struck dead by God, was interpreted as a warning against masturbation. However, later scholars reinterpreted the story of Onan and concluded that his crime was disobeying God's order to fulfill his duty by getting his brother's wife with child. Actually, masturbation is never mentioned in either the Old or New Testaments.

In both Europe and America, women healers were wrongfully accused of being witches and were burned at the stake. As witchcraft gradually lost its reputation as the major cause of madness, medical professionals took control by establishing masturbation as the next symptom of insanity. Naturally, these new priests of medical science had the only remedy. Cruel restraining devices, electrical shocks, deadly injections, and male and female circumcision were used to stop children and adults from touching their own genitals for gratification. This next fact belongs in *Ripley's Believe It or Not:* It wasn't until 1972 that the American Medical Association declared masturbation a normal sexual activity.

While politics can be an art or a science and religion a way to develop spiritual principles, more recently both have been used to deal with people in an opportunistic, manipulative, and power-hungry way. Once a person realizes how the prohibition of masturbation has been used as a strategy to control us, it becomes clear why people are sexually repressed. Many Catholics, Jews, Mormons, Protestants, and Muslims still believe masturbation is a sin. Quite a few of these people are sitting in Congress enacting and supporting laws that directly affect our sexual liberties.

The most common complaint at the top of the list for most married couples is incompatible sex drives. If I could pass a law that says all couples must take a sexual compatibility test before marriage, I would do so. It would also have a clause that says young men and women must be sexual with at least half a dozen partners before choosing one to marry. Most young couples today who have been married for about ten years have lived with the fear of contracting AIDS, so they ended up going steady throughout their twenties. There was little opportunity to experiment with different sex partners.

On top of that, children grow up with a sexual double standard for masturbation. Boys are expected to ejaculate as part of a biological need. Meanwhile, young girls are sexually repressed and masturbation is never mentioned or encouraged because girls can have an unwanted pregnancy once they hit puberty. Once a woman gets married, a sex fairy is supposed to come along, wave a magic wand, and turn her into a sexpot, but the lack of masturbation keeps her from having orgasms in partnersex. The only magic wand I've come across plugs into an outlet. My advice to men married to women who have little interest in sex is to get a

Magic Wand along with my books and read them together. Talk about how to include masturbation in your lives.

As I head into my fourth decade of teaching and advocating the acceptance and advancement of masturbation, many people still think the idea is hysterically funny, and some think it's downright disgusting. Yet more and more people are embracing masturbation for couples. They agree that the repression of masturbation is indeed the bottom line of sexual repression, and that the uninhibited practice of masturbation can often reverse this stifling sexual tyranny. As we become more at home in our sexual bodies, we will enjoy a more lighthearted form of pleasure in our relationships.

Share the good news with all of your close friends: Embracing masturbation is the foundation for mutually orgasmic partnersex. That statement will at least start an interesting conversation, I promise.

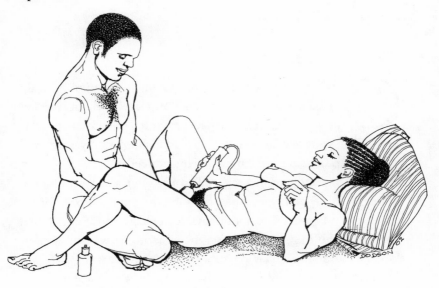

SHE WANTS MORE. *After an hour of hot partnersex, she is still turned on and wants to come again. He is stroking her genitals while she uses the vibrator to have another orgasm. He'll probably get another erection and they'll have another round of penis/vagina intercourse.*

❧ 9 ❧

SEX TOYS

For Couples Who Want to Have Fun

ONE AFTERNOON IN 1965, Grant was getting his scalp massaged by his barber with an electric vibrator when he thought, "This would be great for clitoral stimulation!" That same day he went to a barbershop supply store and bought one. The next evening he introduced me to the Oster vibrator. After applying massage oil to my cunt and warming me up manually, he calmly strapped the vibrator onto the back of his hand. At first I wasn't sure about having an electric machine in bed with us, but his fingers were doing the vibrating. It was still skin on skin, so I thought it was probably okay. The orgasm I had was absolutely amazing, and I gradually accepted the vibrator as a sexual toy to play with from time to time.

In 1970, I showed a drawing of a woman using the same Oster vibrator as part of my second art exhibition. This resulted in a media blackout by reviewers and ended my relationship with the gallery. Convinced I'd discovered that the bottom line of sexual repression is the repression of masturbation, I decided to temporarily leave the art world to become involved with feminism and women's sexual liberation. I began writing straightforward articles about the most effective use of electric vibrators and teaching women how to harness all that energy for sexual pleasure in my workshops.

At the first big NOW sexuality conference in 1973, I had the privilege of introducing electric vibrators to feminists for their orgasmic benefits. My lecture overflowed into the hallway. A year later, I published the first feminist book devoted entirely to the subject of self-pleasuring: *Liberating Masturbation: A Meditation on Selflove.* At that point, I was having difficulty finding electric massagers for my workshops, so I convinced my friend Dell Williams to start a mail-order business at home selling electric vibrators along with my book. The essential ingredients for every workshop was a case of electric vibrators, extension cords, and bottles of massage oil for genital massage and vaginal penetration with our fingers and cucumber dildos.

In 1975, Dell opened the first American erotic boutique for women, called Eve's Garden. Since then, woman-owned sex stores have cropped up across the United States and Europe. These stores have become safe havens where women can get vibrators, dildos, lubricants, books, videos, and any other information they need to explore their sexuality.

Several years into singing the praises of electric vibrators, I became aware of the prejudice against women's using them. Occasionally I would have moments of doubt, wondering if I was getting thousands of women addicted to electric orgasms. And if that was the case, what did it mean? The antivibrator flack came from different sources. First it was women who were hesitant to even try a vibrator for fear it would be the only way they could come. Many of these women were not having orgasms with a partner or with themselves, yet they were concerned about getting hooked on a sex toy. Convinced their orgasms should be the result of a lover's touch, a tongue, or a penis, they preferred to wait for the right man to show up to get them off.

Another segment of dissenters in the seventies who cautioned me against using electric vibrators were women psychologists doing sex therapy. Most of them were dedicated to the idea that if a woman learned how to masturbate by hand, the man in her life could give her an orgasm manually, thus partially fulfilling the romantic image. Today, sex therapists rarely hesitate to recommend a battery or electric vibrator to help a woman overcome her inability to have an orgasm, so we have made some progress.

The last group to raise hell were men who would go to any length to eliminate all electric vibrators and vibrating dildos. Some believed sex toys were instruments of the devil that would destroy their two favorite sacred cows—motherhood and the family. Others were good old boys who had no intention of competing with a machine that, once it was plugged in, could go on and on indefinitely. The very idea that women might want partnersex to include orgasm meant that men would have to change their selfish ways. No longer could they simply ejaculate inside vaginas, then roll over and go to sleep. They felt threatened by vibrators.

But there were always smart men who saw vibrators as an ally, as something that could relieve them of the responsibility of providing her orgasm either manually or orally. These were the men buying the vibrators and bringing them into bed. They wanted their wives and girlfriends to get more turned on and to be able to enjoy partnersex more fully.

Until Joani Blank, the founder of the sex store Good Vibrations, had an exhibition of antique vibrators in the eighties, I had no idea about their long history. In the late 1800s, medical doctors were treating "hysterical" women by giving them hand jobs as an ongoing part of their practice. Female masturbation was forbidden, and since marital sex was limited to vaginal penetration that rarely produced an orgasm, women's sexual frustration was labeled "hysteria" and classified as a chronic condition with many symptoms, like bouts of depression, fainting, nervousness, and generally disrupting family harmony (especially her husband's) with a cantankerous disposition.

To maintain penis/vagina penetration as "normal" sexuality and safeguard men's sexual self-esteem, these bad-tempered or depressed nonorgasmic women were sent to a doctor to be cured of a "disease." The doctors would massage a woman's genitals to orgasm, but they called it relieving her "hysterical paroxysms." In response to physicians' needs, the first electric vibrator was invented as a medical device. These machines reduced the time it took to give a woman an orgasm from about one hour to ten minutes, making doctors' clinical practices far more lucrative. *The Technology of Orgasm* by Rachel Maines details the history of hysteria and the invention of vibrators.

Eventually women were able to buy electric vibrators for home use even before electric irons and vacuum cleaners were invented. Vibrators were sold through catalogs and advertised in respectable women's magazines. But when they began appearing in pornographic films in the twenties, they were no longer made available to the general public. In my opinion, it was just men protecting their sexual self-esteem once again. Vibrators were not only a form of competition, but their use questioned society's definition of "normal sexuality" and was a total upset for Freud's beloved vaginal orgasm. From then on electric vibrators were primarily sold as massage machines to soothe sore muscles, or to stimulate men's scalps to keep them from going bald.

Today, sex toys have become a billion-dollar business. Yet there is still prejudice against using a battery-operated or electric machine for more pleasurable orgasms because this kind of sex features the clitoris. Some states have actually outlawed the sale of dildos and vibrators. Imagine the kind of selfish insecurity that exists in a man who can't bear the thought of his wife's getting a little sexual pleasure from her clitoris instead of his penis.

As the clitoris makes its way into women's definition of healthy female sexuality, I'm often asked the appropriate age for a woman to begin using a vibrator. Without any sexual repression, each woman would experience an easy progression of clitoral contact. In early childhood, she would explore her genitals manually and have the clitoris named by the time she was a few years old. Young girls would enjoy self-stimulation the way boys do. Teenage girls would explore having their clitorises touched by someone else's fingers with an opposite- or same-sex sweetheart. After securing some form of birth control, girls who like boys would begin to have penis/vagina sex. Adding manual clitoral stimulation during intercourse would be natural. In their thirties, some women might want to use a battery-operated or electric vibrator. By their forties, electric vibrators would be a welcome addition for clitoral stimulation.

Unfortunately, this kind of natural progression rarely happens. If a woman has reached her mid- to late twenties with little or no experience of masturbation, I recommend that she jump-start her sexual response with a battery-operated vibrator. If that doesn't work, by all means use an electric, plug-in vibrator. I see no harm for young women who began masturbating with a vibrator, except it might upset a narrow-minded lover who needs to be the source of her orgasm. Why should it matter what type of clitoral stimulation a woman prefers as long as it works—whether she's using her hand, a lover's hand, an electric vibrator, a stream of water in the bathtub, or the spin cycle while leaning up against the washing machine?

Since the seventies I have recommended the Hitachi Magic Wand for massage and sexual pleasure without reimbursement for my endorsement. While other vibrator companies have approached me with business propositions, I felt that their product did not match the quality of the Wand. Officially, the Magic Wand is sold as a body massager, and it's great for soothing sore muscles throughout the body. Its therapeutic vibrations bring a new supply of blood to any area being massaged, including genital engorgement. Vibratex is the current American distributor. The owners said that Mr. Hitachi's son is aware of the role I have played in making his vibrator so popular. I've been told they intend to make me part of the design team for the next generation of Magic Wands.

Although I have nothing against using massage oil and our hands for clitoral stimulation, women who have no history of masturbation consistently say they get tired before they feel anything sexual, so manual stimulation rarely works. Using a battery-operated or electric vibrator will make up for years of sensory deprivation. For a woman who is looking for her first orgasm as an adult, the Magic Wand will awaken a slumbering clitoris by providing strong, steady stimulation for as long as she needs it exactly where it feels best. The vibrator also works wonders for the woman interested in increasing the intensity of her orgasms. She might desire several orgasms during a session of self-loving, or she wants to enjoy stronger orgasms during penetration sex with a partner. An electric vibrator is a must for postmenopausal women who want to revitalize a fading libido.

In order to harness the powerful energy of the Magic Wand vibrator, I suggest starting off with several layers of a soft washcloth or something comparable. As the clitoris adjusts to stronger sensation, the layers of fabric can be reduced over a period of ten to twenty minutes, ending with one layer. Eventually, I wrap a washcloth over the head of the vibrator and attach it with the rubber band from a bunch of broccoli. Some women hold the vibrator above, below, or to one side of the clitoris. Other women like to use the vibrator directly on their clits to have a fast climax, but taking thirty minutes to an hour will build up more sexual tension and produce a fuller orgasm. However, there is no law against the occasional quickie to relieve tension. I call them "maintenance orgasms." Experimentation is always a good idea.

In my opinion, the Magic Wand is to women what Viagra is to men. I've never heard a man apologize for using Viagra in order to enjoy his orgasms. If Bob Dole, the former Republican Senate Majority Leader, can go on television and tell the world he uses Viagra, no woman ever need apologize to anyone for using an electric vibrator. We, too, have the right to enjoy our orgasms and lay claim to our definition of female sexual pleasure, which often includes using a vibrator for direct clitoral stimulation.

Today, I no longer worry about vibrator addiction, just as I doubt many of the accusations about a person's being a sex addict or addicted to pornography. In many of these cases, I believe the accusers are simply jealous because they think the other person is having more fun than they are. Instead of being concerned about sex addiction, the things I worry about in America are poverty, racism, denying women equal rights, lack of sex education, access to contraception, and the right to choose abortion.

Many people still visualize the penis-shaped plastic cheapos when they hear the word "vibrator." These battery-operated vibrators first entered the marketplace back in the sixties and were sold by the millions in drugstores. They are now available in every size and color imaginable. Because they are penis-shaped, a lot of people think they are used for vaginal penetration, but most women use them simply to stimulate their clitorises. Some women prefer the softer vibrations of a battery-operated vibrator. The more popular small battery-operated vibrators are not much larger than a lipstick case. My favorite is the Water Dancer. It delivers a strong vibration and takes only one AA battery. It's great for traveling. Many women now own several vibrators: a battery-operated, an electric, and a rechargeable.

The Japanese battery-operated vibrators like the Rabbit Pearl are big sellers because they look so appealing. The shaft twists and turns and vibrates with pearls rolling around behind clear plastic in the middle of the dildo. A small rabbit with rapidly vibrating ears sits at the base and is meant to stimulate the clitoris. However, the placement of the rabbit's ears doesn't work for me once the shaft is inside my vagina. The twisting shaft doesn't move that much with strong vaginal muscles. After trying it, I ended up using just the rabbit's ears on my clit. An enterprising company tuned into this fact and there is now a sex toy with just the rabbit's vibrating ears. If you are in love with one of these Japanese toys, that's great. Enjoy yourself.

Although it seems like a great idea to have both vaginal penetration and clitoral stimulation in one toy, after years of experimentation, my personal preference is to keep my vaginal penetration separate from the vibrator stimulating my clitoris. This way I have the choice of using different rhythms with either one. The vibrator can be moving rapidly on my clit while I'm doing a slow fuck with a dildo, or vice versa.

Some women prefer the gun-shaped electric vibrators because they tend to be quieter. These women feel more secure vibrating soundlessly when someone else is in the house. However, the gun vibrators have an electromagnetic coil that runs at a very fast speed. It's the same motor that's used in electric shavers and it vibrates too fast for my personal taste. The small attachments deliver a pinpoint-type of stimulation that I find irritating, while other women seem to like it. In my opinion, the large rubber head on the "wand vibrators" spreads the sensations better and the motor creates a slower vibe. Again, if you're having a hot affair with the coil vibrator, continue to enjoy your orgasms.

There are also wand vibrators that are cordless to provide mobility. The Acuvibe holds a fairly long charge, which makes it great for car trips, camping, or an afternoon on a deserted beach. One summer my girlfriend and I took our rechargeable vibrators to the ocean and found a huge, flat rock at the water's edge. We stretched out on the warm smooth surface in the late afternoon sun and had our orgasms with the waves lapping beneath us as we listened to the sound of the surf mingled with the seagulls' cries. There is something very special about being naked and sexual in Mother Nature's living room under a bright blue sky with clouds floating overhead.

One woman who e-mailed me was concerned about using a
vibrator as a crutch, a mechanical quick fix for instant gratification.
Her question—once she uses it, how will she learn not to use it?—
begs a response. Who has the right to decide if a woman has to
learn *not* to use a vibrator. Her lover? Society? Religion? The government? I have always said there is no "right" way to have an
orgasm. Given the pervasive history of female sexual repression, I'd
say every woman deserves all the help she can get. While some
might call an electric vibrator a crutch, I call it a blessing. Try convincing a man the Viagra he's using is a crutch.

A forty-seven-year-old woman who had her first orgasm with
a vibrator couldn't thank me enough. "Searching for an orgasm has
been a lifelong problem and a heavy weight has been lifted off
my shoulders. The orgasms I have now are extremely intense and
so pleasurable. I just had no idea this is what it would feel like
until now."

Another woman who'd been using an electric vibrator for the
past few years wanted to start having vaginal orgasms with her new
boyfriend: "We're very much in love and for the first time in my
life, I want him to give me my orgasm. He has his orgasm during
intercourse, and I'd like to have mine that way, too. What do I do?"

My success rate in teaching a woman how to have an orgasm
from intercourse alone has been zero percent, so I urged her to
incorporate the vibrator into her love affair. Some therapists recommend retiring the vibrator and then spending the next six
months learning to masturbate by hand. This would allow her lover
to be the source of her orgasm with manual clitoral stimulation or
oralsex. More often than not, a woman ends up getting discouraged. She goes back to using the vibrator, but now she feels like
more of a failure. Still, I know of a few cases where women have
learned to do manual stimulation so their partners could get them
off. What's the catch? They tell me their orgasms are not as powerful, but they feel more emotionally satisfied because now their husbands are happier.

I've had a couple of friends who used a vibrator for a few years and then decided to go back to their hands. They already had a history of enjoying manual masturbation, so it was no big deal for them to return to their fingers. They preferred a less intense kind of orgasm and the freedom of not having to plug into an outlet. It was a choice that worked. However, a woman who has had her first orgasms with a vibrator and has continued to do so for years is not likely to learn how to use a lesser form of stimulation.

Like other men, Eric admitted he was angry at first over the thought of being outmatched by a vibrator. But instead of feeling obsolete or threatened, he decided to form an alliance with the vibrator after reading my book *Sex for One*. By focusing more on expanding the art of sexual pleasure, he knew that a woman's orgasmic experience would be even greater if he combined his erotic input while she controlled her clitoral stimulation. His cock gliding slowly in and out of her vagina with the vibrator on her clitoris while his hands caressed her breasts and body would surpass her use of the vibrator alone. The vibrations he could feel on his penis added to his pleasure as well. Cooperation instead of competition was the answer to superior sex for both him and any girlfriend who preferred coming with a vibrator.

Now when Eric talks to his twenty-something friends he says, "Hey guys, how do you think a woman who is consistently orgasmic with a vibrator will feel when you tell her she can't bring that 'thing' into bed with you? When that happens, you've demonstrated that your dick ego is more important to you than her pleasure." He ends by telling each man that including a vibrator into his partnersex will allow him to be the great lover he imagined he already was. It's a very simple principle. Any man who offers sexual pleasure by incorporating the woman's clitoris without conditions will be rewarded with, among other things, her genuine appreciation and affection.

The following letter represents the conflict that a sexually sophisticated woman felt when she first discovered vibrator sex:

I am a forty-eight-year-old female, presently unattached. Recently I wanted to try a vibrator since I had never used one. Assuming I could integrate the Hitachi vibrator (God, I love that thing!) into my repertoire, I began having the most incredible orgasms of my life. They are so much more intense. I have at least three rapid-fire climaxes in five minutes or less before I can slow it down to make it last longer and develop a fantasy. The problem is I can no longer get off with my hand, and I am actually scared that a man will never satisfy me again.

She says the vibrator is giving her the most incredible orgasms of her life and, yes, that's compelling. As for a man satisfying her, the most incredible partnersex orgasms of her life are just around the corner once she uses the vibrator on her clitoris during intercourse. The universal blind spot for women and men is combining vibrator or manual stimulation of the clitoris during penis/vagina sex.

Let me repeat myself: The electric vibrator is to women what Viagra is to men. The pharmaceutical companies are spending billions of dollars on erectile dysfunction drugs for men; women are next. Imagine all the postmenopausal wives having to put up with millions of Viagra-fueled hardons along with their husbands' clumsy attempts at intercourse after years of no action, no sexual skills, and the build up of marital resentments. Many of these wives were relieved to end partnersex. These older couples desperately need a refresher course in Fucking 101 that would include information about the importance of women using an electric vibrator for clitoral stimulation along with adding plenty of additional vaginal lubrication with a massage oil and possibly the use of hormone cream.

Electric vibrators can also be a treat for older men. A man in his early sixties said he picked up his wife's electric vibrator one afternoon, got under the covers, and began moving it on and around his penis. Soon the sensations felt wonderful and he went on to have a big orgasm. Next he discovered he could keep vibrating with or without an erection. The vibrator kept him in a suspended state of high sexual arousal indefinitely. Another man in his seventies told me that due to his health problems, Viagra was not an option. He thanked me for recommending the Magic Wand to his wife. He discovered he can have an orgasm without an erection or ejaculation by using her vibrator while watching X-rated videos. He ordered a second Wand for himself.

A dildo is designed for penetration only and can be made from different materials—highly polished wood, stainless steel, plastic, glass, latex. Artists have even carved dildos from semiprecious stones like jade or onyx. Many are penis-shaped but some are not. My favorite dildos are proudly displayed as works of art on a bookshelf in my living room. I see them as empowered objects that retain the vibrations of each orgasm I've had using them. My pattern is to fall in love with a dildo for a period of time, and then the next thing I know, I'm looking around for a new one. It's sort of like romantic love. When it's over, I just move along and find the next beloved. Sometimes I'll make love to an old favorite and recall the good times we've had.

Many women ask me how to determine the best size for a dildo. Personally, I prefer a range of sizes. But if you're looking for Mr. Just Right, get a large cucumber or zucchini and carve it down gradually, putting it inside your vagina at different stages until you discover what feels best. Then measure the length and diameter and go on-line or to a sex store and buy your match made in heaven. Do yourself a favor and buy a dildo made with the best-quality materials: latex, silicone, glass, steel, or some other quality material. Cyberskin actually feels like flesh. The brightly colored, translucent, jelly-type dildos burn the inside of some women's vaginas, mine included. A few sex stores recommend using them with a condom, but that can become a nuisance.

Betty's Barbell is one of my favorite dildos. I finally got around to designing a sex toy that doubles as a vaginal exerciser. The prototype was used in my workshops and private sessions, proving its benefits before I manufactured them to sell on my website. The

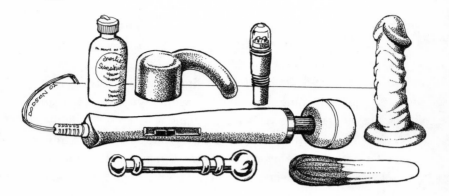

TOYS FOR LOVERS. *These sex toys are my favorites.
Instructions on the best way to enjoy them can be found on my website,
www.bettydodson.com. The dildo on the bottom right is a zucchini
customized with a vegetable peeler. Gradually increasing the size of her
inexpensive vegetable dildo is a safe way for a young woman to practice
self-penetration.*

design is similar to a small barbell with a larger ball on one end and
a smaller ball on the other. Made of a highly polished stainless steel,
it's indestructible and very attractive. The smooth surface feels great
sliding in and out of a well-oiled vagina. Betty's Barbell weighs
nearly a pound and the length is six and three-quarter inches. Once
inserted into the vagina, the weight keeps it in place, leaving both
hands free so you can keep a vibrator humming away on your clitoris while squeezing the pelvic floor muscles.

We sometimes forget that a healthy body is the best sex toy
available. Locating and exercising your pelvic floor muscle will
enhance your orgasm with yourself as well as during partnersex.
The same muscle also ensures bladder control and maintains vaginal health. This is true for men as well. The pubococcygeal, or PC,
muscle is like a sling that attaches to the front of the pubic bone
and goes across the pelvic floor circling the anus. One way to locate
the PC muscle is to abruptly stop and start the flow of urine. A
more dramatic way is to insert a finger inside your vagina and

squeeze the PC muscle. To exercise the PC muscle, *lift up* and relax, do not bear down.

Betty's Barbell is a resistance device that increases the benefit of doing what has long been known as Kegel exercises. The best assurance for continuing is to combine your workout with masturbation and end with an orgasm using the Barbell as a dildo. Once the exercise is associated with sexual pleasure, each woman will discover her individual preference. Consciously working the PC muscle while masturbating promotes vaginal lubrication and clearly enhances the pleasures of orgasm. Young women who are penetration virgins can start with the small end of Betty's Barbell and gradually open their vaginal barrel to avoid painful first-time intercourse.

Men who are anal penetration virgins also need to start small and gradually build up the size, but a word of caution: Anything that goes inside the anus has to be a dildo with balls or a butt plug with a flared base on one end. This is so the little bugger won't wander off into the dark recesses of your lower bowel. So, if you are using my Barbell anally, be sure to keep a good grip on one end of it. It's amazing what some folks will put up their butts when in the throes of some serious anal loving. Remember those plastic penis-shaped cheapos I mentioned? I've seen an X-ray that showed one of them lodged inside a man's descending colon; it had to be surgically removed.

Dildo penetration provides a nice full vaginal or anal feeling that many people enjoy. When making love to yourself, remember to also use plenty of extra lubrication for the most sensual penetration. Too often women have the idea that their own lubrication should be sufficient. This is ridiculous. Sometimes I've been turned on and there was a minimum of wetness and other times I've been doing the dishes not thinking about sex when I felt moisture in my vagina and discovered I was lubricating. In this culture, we think a wet pussy is the equivalent of a man's hardon, but a woman's clitoris also gets erect when she's aroused. I'm constantly telling people to use plenty of lubrication for masturbation and partnersex. As my friend Isadora Alman said, sex education can be summed up in two words: lubrication and communication.

When it comes to masturbation or manual sex, I much prefer oil to a water-based lube. For couples who are fluid-bonded, oil is more sensuous for all kinds of penetration sex. ("Fluid-bonded" is a term for couples who have agreed to always use condoms with a water-based lube when they have sex with other partners, but with one another, it's skin on skin using massage oil.) Most of the massage oils sold in health food stores are safe. Avoid edible mixtures that have sugar, which can cause a vaginal yeast infection. Petroleum-based products like Vaseline are said to build up on mucous membranes. I'm using a massage oil called Charlie Sunshine made from food-grade natural oils that's available on my website. While I don't have anything against using saliva for penetration, it usually dries out too quickly.

For couples using condoms, you must use a water-based lube in order not to break down the latex. There are a number of brands to choose from, so try several and make your own choice. The latest technology is a silicone lube called Eros, but I'm not sure how safe it is. In my opinion, the jury is still out on the long-term effects of liquid silicone inside the body. I like the thicker Probe, which has a citrus preservative. When a water-based lube gets sticky, you can bring the slippery consistency back by using a few drops of water or saliva. When it gets too thin add more lube. Some women have an allergic reaction to water-based lubes and latex.

For ten years I was a member of the advisory board for Xandria, one of the largest distributors of sex toys. They did a survey titled "Toys in the Sheets" about who was buying from their catalog. Contrary to the myth that sex toys are kinky fetishes for people living on the sexual fringe, the survey showed that the majority of people who used them are Middle Americans. Xandria's typical sex-toy user was a married, monogamous, college-educated, white, Christian woman in her thirties who voted Republican. She had children at home and a family income greater than $40,000 a year. There was an enormous range of people using sex toys and nearly half were men. They included every race, religion (except Muslim), income bracket, and age group from teens to seniors. Once I saw that only 9 percent of the buyers used sex toys during partnersex, I knew the next direction my work had to take.

Today I keep a big silver trunk in my living room full of every imaginable sex toy available. It makes a great conversation piece whenever I open it up and show the contents to friends or clients. We then spend some time going through my treasure chest while I do show-and-tell about the variety of grown-up toys that are available. I've got all the expensive Japanese vibrators with little animals on the side. They all run off batteries with varying speeds. Some toys are vibrating eggs that fit inside the vagina and can be remotely controlled by a lover. There is a double dildo that can be used by two women, two men, or a man and a woman. I'll give you a moment to figure that one out.

The buttplugs go from small to quite large and some vibrate. There are several latex beads of varying sizes strung together that are slowly pulled out of a buttyhole just as a person is coming. There are cockrings made of leather, plastic, rubber, and metal that some men wear to enhance erections and others wear because they look good. There is a penis pump. I've got satin blindfolds, soft restraints, and a set of Sport Sheets that have Velcro bondage built into the sheet. There are cute little string whips and a very expensive large one made from strips of soft suede that makes a wonderful sound but doesn't deliver intense pain. All of this is in addition to at least a dozen Magic Wands. There's a box of little Water Dancers, a box of batteries, several dozen Betty's Barbells, and lots of Charlie Sunshine massage oil. When it comes to bringing a last-minute gift, I never have a problem.

We all know how confusing it can be to buy a sex toy from a website with a huge selection of different items. Pardon my commercial, but if you want to keep it simple, be sure to visit my website, where I have a handful of products that have been personally tested and selected by me, along with my erotic sex education videos and books. I'm also linked to my favorite on-line stores with every conceivable sex toy plus novelty items. Life is much too short to deprive yourself of another moment of the additional pleasures and earthly delights that are just a click away.

While I am constantly recommending the use of lubricants for sex, I also make sure clients and visitors to my website know that manual sex alone or assisting your partner during masturbation is far more sensuous with massage oil than with a water-based lube. *The only time I recommend using a water-based lube is when condoms are involved.* I fully understand and support the importance of condoms for safer sex while dating. However, once a couple is monogamous and the woman is using some other kind of birth control or post-menopausal, they can embrace the sensuality of naked, wet sex using a massage oil. When I think of all the young couples who are monogamous and still using condoms and water-based lube, it breaks my heart. When I think of all the Viagra-fueled erections plunging into thousands of postmenopausal vaginas without massage oil, I could cry.

Although I've always advised against using petroleum-based lubes, if you've been using Vaseline for masturbation, don't worry, your clit or dick won't drop off. My main objection to Vaseline is that it's a slow drag rather than a slippery slide. Any nut or vegetable oil is far more sensuous.

Many of my friends and I fucked our way through the sexual revolution of the sixties dipping into big pink cans of Albolene that had petroleum listed in the ingredients. Most of my girlfriends were on the pill. At the time, I was wearing a diaphragm lined with a spermicidal jelly containing nonoxynol-9, which killed off invading bacteria. While enjoying multiple partners I never had an STD and my diaphragm remained intact. In the seventies I switched over to an almond massage oil that was based on Edgar Casey's formula.

Again my nonoxynol-9-lined diaphragm didn't deteriorate and I remained disease free. Today I'm using Charlie Sunshine's unscented massage oil, which is made from food-grade vegetable oils. That means you can suck a clit or a cock that's covered with this oil and there's no bad taste. Vaginal or anal penetration with fingers, dildos, or penises is always more delicious with a clean vegetable or nut oil for couples who are monogamous or fluid-bonded.

❧ 10 ❧

ORGASMS FOR TWO

Intercourse with Clitoral Stimulation

WHEN MY THERAPIST TOLD ME I had to work at making my marriage work, I hated the idea. If I had married the right man, everything, including our sex life, would have fallen into place for the happily-ever-after part. Or so I'd been raised to believe. Instead of growing up on the stuff of fairy tales, I would have been better off hearing the truth: Relationships don't work and life isn't fair. Once a couple accepts this reality, they can agree to sit down and discuss what they can do to make their partnership work. Along with maintaining ongoing negotiations to deal with life's changes, another important element in diffusing the natural conflict that exists in every partnership is a couple's ability to enjoy orgasms for two.

If there were ever healing moments that are universal, I believe it's the tender feelings couples have for each other after sharing orgasmic sex. As they lie together in each other's arms, they are filled with gratitude for the pleasure that lingers in their bodies, renewing their appreciation for each other. Genuinely liking our partners and showing it with an abundance of affection will last far beyond the short shelf life of all those idealized versions of romantic love combined.

Learning how to share orgasms involves skills that must be learned and then practiced. Let me make an analogy between orgasmic partnersex and ballroom dance. Without any instruction, a couple will stand on the dance floor and move from side to side in one place with little style or grace. The tango is a hot, gorgeous dance everyone loves to watch and fantasize about doing, but its sizzle comes only with training. We would never expect a couple to be able to tango together "naturally" just because they are in love. At some point they need someone to show them a few basic steps.

Continuing the dance analogy, in traditional ballroom dancing, the man leads, but in partnersex, they can agree to take turns. The point is that who leads, who follows, and when to take turns is determined beforehand. When a man leads he learns how to place his arms and hands to signal his partner with subtle pressure before he makes a move. She learns to read his signals and easily follows him. The music determines the rhythm. They also know in advance whether they will be doing the salsa or western line dancing. Once they learn the basic moves their confidence allows them to be carried away by the joy of moving together with the music.

Similar to choosing a style of dance, it's best to experiment with different sexual positions in order to discover the ones you both like. Make sure the position includes the woman's choice for the kind of clitoral contact she prefers. She might want it from her hand, a battery-operated vibrator, or an electric vibrator. If she can climax from indirect clitoral stimulation, again certain positions will be better for her. For those couples who prefer having the man doing the clitoral touching, the woman will need to give directions until he becomes familiar with her pattern of masturbation.

If a woman wants to introduce something new to her lover, it's not a good idea to discuss it right before having sex. A client who had learned how to come with a vibrator went into great detail about how she wanted to use it during partnersex while her lover was lying there with a hardon lusting for an orgasm. He was so frustrated that he barely heard a word she said. Once he came, they were able to talk about what she wanted to try with him. Several hours later they had sex again. This time they were both ecstatic when she had a huge orgasm using the vibrator while they were fucking.

Some of my fondest memories are the times I've had in-depth conversations with a lover after we've shared orgasms. When one of us did something that was a little different and we both enjoyed the sensation it created, going over it when the details are still fresh means we can refine our moves to make it even better the next time. Affectionate hugging and kissing, manual or oral sex, slow penetration, the erotic dance itself, and cuddling afterward—it's worth spending an hour or more to enjoy mutually orgasmic partnersex. A four-hour weekend afternoon is still one of my favorites.

The positions that work best will depend on the couple's age, body type, and range of motion. A good approach is to be playful, creative, and experimental while both of you talk freely. One important requirement of any position is that it be comfortable. When fatigue sets in, something hurts, or a muscle is strained, the sexual buildup for either a man or woman will inevitably get derailed. Some of the following positions will work equally well for lesbians who are into strapping on a dildo.

MAN ON TOP

The good old missionary position is what most people think of as "normal" sex. As long as I'm not required to have my orgasm this way, I can enjoy the warm-up stage of partnersex reclining on my back while he massages my genitals. Once he's fully erect, shallow penetration is erotic, especially when he teases me by moving just the head of his penis in and out at the opening of my vagina, building my level of desire for deeper penetration. When a man leans forward on his arms to penetrate deeper there is still enough room for a woman to reach down and do her clitoris with fingers or a small battery-operated vibrator. When a couple is belly to belly in the man-on-top position, a few women get indirect clitoral stimulation and can climax by grinding up against their partner's body.

One couple I worked with liked a hard-pounding fuck because they had never known anything else. They both believed she should be able to come from his penis in the missionary position. We have seen this style of sex ad nauseam for the past thirty years in movies and porn. Although her clitoris was getting indirectly stimulated every time he banged into her body, it was not enough for her to come consistently. Once she was able to add her own clitoral stimulation and they slowed down, more subtle erotic sensations emerged. He still moves faster just before he has his orgasm, but she discovered it was best when she slowed down right in front of hers.

When a man does oralsex as foreplay and then climbs on top to fuck a woman hard and fast, I call this old-fashioned sex. I believe the coital imperative with vigorous thrusting stems from our culture's lack of sexual skills and knowledge about making direct contact with the clitoris during intercourse. For some men the fast friction fuck is a continuation of a childhood masturbation pattern. A few guys are sadistic and enjoy using their penis as a weapon, as if they're trying to pierce through the woman in an egotistical display of masculine power.

In some X-rated videos we often see men pushing a woman's legs back over her head to get more access to her pussy. Although it makes a good camera shot, she's literally pinned down. If not being able to move turns a woman on, then there's no problem. But many women find this position uncomfortable to hold for any length of time. An alternative would be a woman wrapping her legs around a man's back and locking them together by crossing her ankles. When I do this position it's like visiting an old friend. It's fun as long as I know I don't have to have my orgasm this way.

WOMAN ON TOP

Women who can climax from indirect clitoral stimulation often say getting on top is the best position for them. In my early twenties I discovered that I, too, could climax more consistently on top. One summer when I was home visiting my family in Kansas, I had just started a new affair. He was home from college, too, visiting his folks, so neither of us had any privacy. We had a lot of sex in the backseat of his car parked in a wheat field. The most comfortable position was when I sat on top of him, pressing my clitoris into his body each time I thrust my hips forward. The first time I saw the word "autoerotic" I thought it meant having sex in a car.

When casual sex was abundant in the sixties and seventies, I challenged the sexual double standard by breaking free from the old rules about appropriate sexual behavior for women. Men were encouraged to be sexually assertive while I was supposed to be passive. They could have multiple partners while I had to choose one man. No longer blinded by romantic love and as a sexual feminist in rebellion, I gave myself permission to claim the same sexual freedom that successful bachelors enjoyed. No wonder so many men adore sport fucking. It was exciting, and even if the sex wasn't that good, I learned something new about human sexuality and myself each time.

One important discovery was realizing that as long as the man controlled how we had sex, I was dependent on his technique. But if I got on top, ran the fuck, and did my own clitoral stimulation, casual partnersex was more enjoyable. Being on top made it possible for me to oil both of our genitals to get the slippery sensuous feeling and do slow penetration. When he tried to push inside too deep, I controlled the depth of his thrusting by raising my hips. I could also establish a nice, leisurely motion to slow down those men who thought faster and harder was good sex. Most guys were grateful when I stated or demonstrated my sexual preferences and took control of my clitoral stimulation. A few were threatened, and occasionally a guy would get angry, but it was never a problem because there was always safety in numbers at sex parties.

The female superior position also makes it easy for a man to use his fingers or thumb for clitoral stimulation. Or she can easily use her fingers or a battery-operated or electric vibrator on her clitoris during intercourse while using her leg muscles to move up and down on his penis. Since she'll be sitting in full view, she can't be self-conscious about the appearance of her body. Women who don't like the way their breasts or bellies look can wear sexy lingerie. Believe me, most men could care less about how a woman's belly looks while she's vibrating on his dick. He will be too busy loving the intensity of her authentic turn-on as she rides him all the way to orgasm.

RIGHT ANGLE POSITION

This is a very comfortable position for both the woman and man. She lies on her back with her knees bent while he is lying on his side with his body at a ninety-degree angle to hers (see page 2). The leg positions will vary among couples, but usually she has one leg under his and the other one over him. Either the man or woman can provide manual clitoral stimulation while they're fucking. It's also perfect if she wants to use the wand-type vibrator with longer handles. He can easily reach her breasts for massage or nipple play. They can also see each other's faces and bodies and both have complete freedom to move their pelvises with ease.

This will always be one of my favorite positions since it's how I first experienced my clitoris being touched during intercourse. I'll never forget the sexual charge that surged through my body when Grant lightly fluttered his fingers on my clit while he slowly glided his hard cock in and out of my eager cunt. The sensation was incredible as I climbed higher and higher, sucking in air until I wailed as my body convulsed with the biggest orgasm I'd ever experienced. It was even better when I took control of my own clitoral stimulation, because now I could slow down or speed up according to what I wanted and needed for my orgasm.

Another position we loved when my bed was about fourteen inches off the floor was when I was lying on my back with Grant kneeling on the floor at the edge of the bed. I could let my folded legs relax and fall open. Either of us could easily do manual clit stim while fucking and watching each other's bodies respond to pleasure. Many beds today need a small ladder to climb up into. When a bed is high off the floor, I can lay my upper body over the edge and enjoy vaginal penetration from behind. For the most part, a futon on the floor saw the most sexual action in my apartment until the end of the nineties, when I returned to using my bed, which is now twenty-four inches off the floor.

LEG UP SIDE POSITION

I thought of calling this "The Horizontal Flamingo" after the bird that stands on one leg. This position is very good with a wand vibrator. The woman is lying on her side with her top leg pulled up toward her chest enough to expose her genitals. She rests her top leg on a pillow or two. The bottom leg is stretched out straight between his legs as he kneels on the bed with his body upright. The Magic Wand vibrator can be placed in between the supporting pillows. This requires some experimentation to find the best position and angle for the vibrator relative to the height of the pillows. The man will primarily be using his thigh muscles in this position to slowly thrust into her vagina, so he will need to have some degree of leg strength.

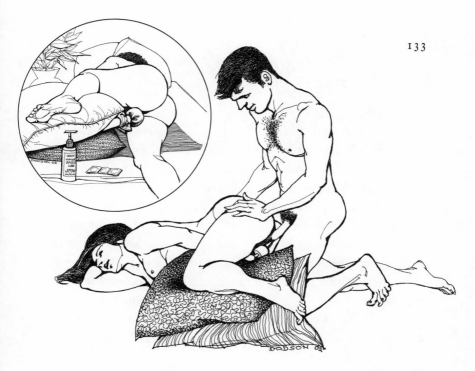

LEG UP SIDE POSITION. *The woman is lying on her side with her top leg pulled up toward her chest and resting on two or more pillows. Her bottom leg is stretched out straight between her partner's legs. He kneels on the bed and moves in close up against the pillows. The Magic Wand is placed between the pillows while she holds on to the handle with one hand. The pillows are arranged for comfort.*

This position recently entered my partnersex repertoire with Eric. For both of us, penetration in the side position is exquisite and very intense. We talked it over, and he believes it's because laying on my side changes the contact between his penis and my vagina. When I'm on my back, the curve of his penis matches the curve of my vagina. On my side, the curves are in opposition, which creates a completely different sensation, making our genital connection feel even more intensely sensuous.

Like most men, Eric is a visual creature, and he sometimes has to close his eyes to keep from coming because the side position looks so hot. Instead of turning my head to see him, I keep my eyes closed and stay focused on what I'm feeling, fantasizing, or both. Sometimes he carefully separates my ass cheeks or gently adds support to my top thigh with one hand. Both are very erotic sensations. Along with his graceful fucking motion, he can simultaneously rub my ass using circular movements with an oiled hand.

As I lift my pelvis slightly to meet each of his deep, unhurried thrusts I can also control the vibrator pressure on my clitoris. Further along into fucking, when I'm fully aroused, the spongy head of his cock gently pressing against my uterus produces extraordinary sensations. Sometimes I squeeze and release my PC muscles, and other times I focus on keeping the pelvic floor muscles totally relaxed. It's a real challenge not to tighten the muscles when it feels so good, but if I stay relaxed, I often feel more exquisite erotic sensations. However, as I head toward climax, the muscles tighten uncontrollably.

There are times when he's close to coming and, instead of pulling out, he pushes all the way inside my vagina and holds still. This avoids any further friction on the sensitive rim of his glans while allowing me to continue vibrating my clitoris and getting a cunt charge as we stay connected. At that point, I can squirm down on his hardon while adding pressure with my vibrator to sustain my arousal. I have actually been able to come like this. When his approaching orgasmic feelings subside and he starts pumping again, I can either start climbing toward more sexual delights and come again or ride the waves of pleasure from my first orgasm while he goes for his climax. The Horizontal Flamingo remains at the top of our list of favorites for fancy fucking with a Magic Wand.

VAGINAL REAR ENTRY POSITION

A lot of women have a problem with vaginal rear entry because they feel it's too "animalistic," but that's exactly why I like it. After all, we are human animals. When a woman is on all fours it's often called doggie style. This allows the deepest penetration, so a man must be gentle and careful not to shove his cock in up to the hilt immediately, especially if he's built large. The biggest problem is when a woman is kneeling on all fours, adding any kind of clitoral contact means she'll have to hold herself up with one arm. This can quickly become tiresome.

One version of doggie that I dislike is a man bending over a woman's back trying to reach around and make clitoral contact or penetrating more deeply. Not only does she have to support his weight, but it also limits their range of motion. When his body is slammed up against hers it restricts their pelvic movements. Doggie is much nicer when there is a little space between bodies so they both have room to move. When I'm behind my partner doing the penetrating, sometimes I hold the dildo still and encourage him or her to do the moving, so they can get the depth and the rhythm they want. The same is true when a man holds still and lets the woman move back and forth on his penis instead of always doing the thrusting.

THE KNEE-CHEST POSITION

This position, with vaginal rear entry, allows a woman to rest her upper body on the bed. With her head turned to one side, she can use a pillow for support. This leaves both hands free and makes it much easier for her to reach down between her legs with one hand to add manual or battery vibrator stimulation. However, with a Wand vibrator, it's a bit difficult to manage the longer handle when the woman is on a bed or the floor. Once we solved the problem of how to deal with the longer handle on the Wand vibrator, the following position has become another one of our favorites. Still, this one depends on individual bed heights as well as the length of each man's legs.

KNEE-CHEST POSITION ON
THE EDGE OF THE BED

The man stands behind the woman while she kneels on the edge of the bed with her lower legs hanging off from about mid-calf down. The handle of the Wand is held on the outside of the bed pointing down toward the floor. This way she can hold the vibrator with one or two hands while getting just the right kind of movement for clitoral stimulation. There is a certain amount of endurance required of the woman in order to hold this position for a long period of time, however whenever her legs get tired, they can change positions. She can adjust the height of her vagina by spreading her legs apart or bringing them closer together. He can facilitate penetration by adjusting his height, narrowing or widening his stance, and bending his knees.

The knee-chest position still gives some freedom of pelvic movement, but I usually focus more on using my pelvic floor muscle as his penis slowly glides in and out of my vagina. Eric sways gently forward and back, keeping his hips under him at all times. He is not swinging his spine back and forth to create the traditional thrust. Instead, his entire body is in motion, utilizing the least amount of effort and maintaining a higher degree of control. As always, his oiled hands are massaging my behind. Once again, it's easy for him to spread my ass cheeks in this position, making me feel delightfully vulnerable. The combination of these sweet sensations turns me into a little sex pig that can't get enough.

During our warm-up, I want vaginal rear entry to start with shallow penetration gradually going deeper. Even though we've discussed this, sometimes he inadvertently presses his cockhead against my uterus too soon and it doesn't feel good. Whenever this happens before I'm ready, I simply lean forward and pull away from him. But once sexual arousal pumps blood into the lining of my uterus, it lifts up, which creates more space. That's when I want all

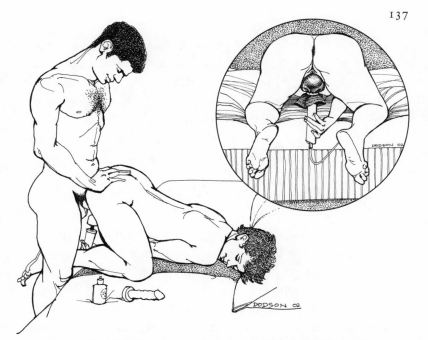

EDGE OF THE BED. *Depending on the height of the bed, a woman kneeling on the edge makes vaginal or anal penetration very easy and sensual. A pillow can support her head and neck if desired. A towel helps to protect bedspreads and sheets. The insert shows the vibrator handle being held on the outside of the bed.*

of him I can get. At that point, I can meet his thrusts by backing up onto to his erect cock. He always maintains a measured rhythm.

Traditionally, men have a tendency to speed up dramatically, overly excited when they think a woman is about to come. This behavior will disrupt her climb to orgasm. What was working before has changed and she now feels pressured to come. Being a steady drummer allows her to speed up just a little bit in front of her orgasm. In sex, changes made gradually usually work better than sudden shifts.

After I'm fully satisfied, I'll tell him to go ahead and have his orgasm when he's ready. At that point he stops all forms of control and goes for what he wants. As he approaches his orgasm, and just before he ejaculates, I can feel his penis swell. With a good hard come he howls like an unholy beast as his orgasm explodes inside me. His youthful energy is exciting and very intense. On a few occasions, one of his dramatic orgasms has turned me on so much that I press the vibrator into my clit and squeeze out several more thrills and chills because I'm already primed for pleasure.

SPOONS

My girlfriend came up with an alternate name for "spoons" because it's one of her favorites. She calls it "Tired Doggie." Although this position hasn't been in my repertoire for quite awhile, a lot of couples sleep together front to back. We call it spoons after how we stack our silverware in the drawer.

Many a woman has been awakened with a firm erection poking her in the back. She will either pull away in disgust, or push back into him, signaling her interest. If he's got a fairly large cock, vaginal penetration can be achieved quite easily in this position. Otherwise she will have to double over to make her genitals more accessible to him. Her hand can be pressed against her clitoris in between her legs or she can raise one leg to use a battery-operated vibrator. Some women use this position as a warm-up before switching to one that provides the kind of clitoral stimulation they prefer.

There are an infinite number of variations on all of these positions, as well as many others, like standing up or sitting in a chair or a woman on top facing away from her partner. All of these can include using a battery-operated or electric vibrator. There are also different types of sex swings that are great, especially for pregnant women or older people with painful hip joints or bad backs. Most important is to experiment by moving around until both of you find the most comfortable position for your bodies. There is no special magic in any one position, and most couples find several that work and then rotate them. If a couple is completely happy with one position and it always produces mutual orgasms, there's nothing wrong with staying true to old faithful. Occasionally changing to something new spices up partnersex, but not always.

Most couples have a timing problem. Women invariably take much longer than men to warm up and have an orgasm. Sometimes I spend fifteen minutes or so vibrating before Eric and I have partnersex. That way I get to have more quality time fucking with him when I'm in a higher state of arousal. Otherwise, we can be fucking for an hour or more and just when he's close to ejaculating, I'm beginning my climb toward ecstasy. That little headstart makes the time we fuck together much hotter. There have been hundreds of times I've heard women say, "Just as it's feeling good, he comes." I suggest women get themselves turned on before they start fucking.

A few couples have learned to have consistent simultaneous orgasms. However, if they expect this to happen every time, it can put a lot of pressure on the woman. We already know that for the most part men are more or less assured of coming during intercourse, while it's much more difficult for women to climax. If their timing isn't perfect, she will be the one who doesn't get to have an orgasm.

TWO WOMEN

There are a variety of ways women can share orgasms for two. In the seventies we were doing a lot of oralsex, but once dental dams or some kind of barrier like Saran Wrap was needed, I much preferred doing manual and vibrator sex. Still, many of my lesbian friends who are committed couples and don't have to worry about health issues say oralsex is their favorite. This is also true for many straight and bisexual women. Oral sex done well provides an ideal form of direct clitoral stimulation that's soft and wet. It also allows a woman to focus entirely on what she's feeling without having to reciprocate simultaneously by doing something in return for her partner.

SIXTY-NINE

In this position both partners are doing oralsex to the other at the same time. This was always more successful for me with women than with men. While sixty-nine can be fun occasionally, I would often lose track of my own arousal and began to focus on my partner. Or if I got caught up in getting close to coming, I would forget to keep doing my partner. The couple of times it worked when both of us were completely in sync all the way to simultaneous orgasms were spectacular. For the most part, however, sixty-nine is confusing, with too much going on all at the same time.

My favorite way to share orgasms with a woman is masturbating with a vibrator while we take turns heightening each other's orgasm with massage and vaginal or anal penetration. When we want to use the same vibrator, we decide who will take control first. The one on the bottom leads by putting the vibrator where it feels best for her and goes for what she wants. The woman on top has to follow the vibrator and position her clitoris to get what she wants. Then we take turns. Women have been so heavily conditioned to sacrifice pleasure to please their partners and "avoid being selfish" that sharing the same vibrator is a great way to practice being self-full.

The concept of taking turns is sexually healing for women. One of the most important principles of orgasms for two is the ability to totally focus on what I'm feeling in my body without any concern for my partner when I'm on the edge of coming. If it's my turn, I have to be able to seize the moment without any reservations. Before I can do this I must trust that my partner will do the same when it's his or her turn to have an orgasm.

TWO MEN

For the most part, gay men are the most sexually sophisticated group when it comes to getting what they want and need in partnersex. Throughout America's sexual revolution, gay men friends were often my inspiration for enjoying advanced forms of sexual expression. In saying that, I don't mean all gay men are sexually uninhibited. Some have many of the same problems that we all struggle with—from self-esteem issues to illusions about romantic love and looking for Mr. Right. Providing they are comfortable with their own sexuality, most gay men are interested in having multiple partners. However, there are couples that choose to be monogamous, especially since the onset of AIDS. In the seventies, during the heyday of sex parties, watching two uninhibited gay men fucking was captivating. I, too, wanted partnersex to be an exchange between two sexually motivated equals moving their bodies like professional dancers toward orgasm.

Looking back over my history of combining clitoral stimulation with intercourse, there were very few men like Grant who encouraged me to do myself. I'm aware of how difficult it is for a woman to make the breakthrough of using her fingers without her partner's initial support. In the seventies, when I was having casual sex with men at sex parties, some guys would push my hand away. I'd just get up off their dicks and move along. Yet even when I was dating a man who embraced manual clit stimulation, it still remained a challenge to introduce an electric vibrator. Maybe it was because a machine seemed more threatening than fingers. It was easier to see fucking as foreplay, and to use my vibrator after we had intercourse and he was long gone. When I had my first affair with a woman, vibrators were a given and we totally embraced them as part of our sexual sharing.

By the time Eric showed up, I had no qualms about including an electric vibrator the first time we had partnersex. He also came to me pro-vibrator. The fact that he is my apprentice gives me far more sexual power than most women have in their relationships and marriages. His focused drive to develop and perfect different forms for creating pleasure combined with my sexual experience and years of teaching sexual pleasure has created an extraordinary opportunity. We have been able to explore heterosexuality combining the use of an electric vibrator with complete freedom— viewing it as desirable and natural. I know there are thousands of women who hesitate to incorporate their electric vibrators into partnersex. Try it. You'll love it. So will he. Then drop me a note with all the details of your newly found pleasures.

When sexuality is no longer kept separate from other aspects of society, the free flow of sex information will gradually establish orgasms for two in pairbonds of all sexual persuasions. Contrary to what the song says, "A good man nowadays is hard to find," it's up to each woman to know what she likes and how she likes it. Once we are able to state our sexual desires—first to our partner, then to our friends, and finally to anyone who's interested—we'll discover that "A good man nowadays is created."

❧ 11 ❧

ESPECIALLY FOR MEN

World-Class Lovers

T O EVERY SMART MAN who has ever asked "What do women want?" I can only answer that sexual desires will differ from woman to woman and depend upon her age. When I was a romance junkie in my early twenties, I went along with whatever kind of sex each boyfriend did as long as he was cute and said he loved me. When I got married I was more concerned with financial security and a loving relationship than sex. After I got divorced and began logging in a little sexual experience with different men, I was able to name several things I enjoyed about sex. By the time I reached forty I was a sexually sophisticated woman who looked for specific qualities to indicate whether a person would be a good lover.

Although society doesn't reward sexually experienced women, I get a lot of personal satisfaction in knowing what I want when it comes to sex. It's a pleasure to be with a man who is self-assured, confident in his ability to get erect and maintain his erection long enough to enjoy the dance of erotic love. If he's not a cocksman, he has mastered oral and manual skills. He has a sensitive touch and never hesitates to ask how I like my clitoris touched. He is never in a hurry. Before touching my clitoris, he always applies some kind of lubrication. When entering my vagina, he savors slow penetration. He supports my orgasm without claiming it as his own creation and totally approves when I take control of my clitoral stimulation. When I want to use a vibrator, he doesn't feel threatened. When I desire penetration while I'm vibrating, he is happy to oblige by using his penis, a finger, or a dildo. After we have shared orgasms, he enjoys spending some quality time snuggling. He likes to talk about sex and explore ways to make it better, and is willing to share some of his fantasies.

Of course I could go on and on for pages covering a multitude of nonsexual qualities that are worth their weight in gold—like intelligence, thoughtfulness, a sense of humor, being affectionate, and the ability to share aspects of his inner life. As for appearance, the most handsome man can turn ugly quickly because of his selfish ways and a homely man can become beautiful because of his generous spirit. With a little maturity, I was far less dedicated to muscular pecs and ass than I had been in my youth.

Nowadays, when it comes to discussing sex, "technique" has practically become a dirty word. Women would rather speak of love and guys have to act like they already know everything. Men have told me that when they use the word "technique" their girlfriends often accuse them of being "too clinical." Women have said when they suggest reading a specific sex book their boyfriends get defensive. So what if we discussed a few sexual skills as if we're talking about how to improve your golf swing, or your three-point shot. After all, few golfers or basketball players would have any problem spending time practicing or taking lessons for these activities.

Let's begin with what I consider to be the first basic requirement for a world-class male lover—the ability to easily get erect. Conscious masturbation is the key to getting and keeping an erection. This is rarely a problem for most guys when they are young and fighting off getting a woody. But as men age, the arteries narrow, blood thickens, and it takes a bit more time and effort to get an erection. If you're in your twenties, quickies are training you to come fast and will interfere with your ability to enjoy erotic love to its fullest. If you are in your forties, those two-minute hand jobs in the morning shower are not circulating your sex energy fully.

Wilhelm Reich once stated that how a person feels about masturbation is how they really feel about sex in general. Back in "the good old days" of casual sex, I used to determine whether or not a guy would be fun in bed by asking how he felt about masturbation. The ones who said they never had to masturbate or they only did it to relieve sexual tension were eliminated immediately. Trial and error taught me that many of those hot-looking Romeos were just using a woman's vagina for masturbation. A few women can come fast like some guys, but in all the years I've listened to women talk about sex, the most common complaint is that intercourse doesn't last long enough.

LEARNING EJACULATORY CONTROL

Most young men ejaculate quickly when they first become sexually active with a partner. Men who want to make partnersex last longer learn how to delay ejaculation by training themselves to sustain higher levels of arousal through the practice of masturbation. When I asked Grant how he learned to keep his hardon, he said that besides being an avid masturbator, fear motivated him. He grew up when condoms were difficult to obtain. If you were lucky enough to get laid, holding off as long as possible and then pulling out was the primary form of birth control. Coitus interruptus is still common today, but most of us know that a man's precome has enough sperm to cause a pregnancy.

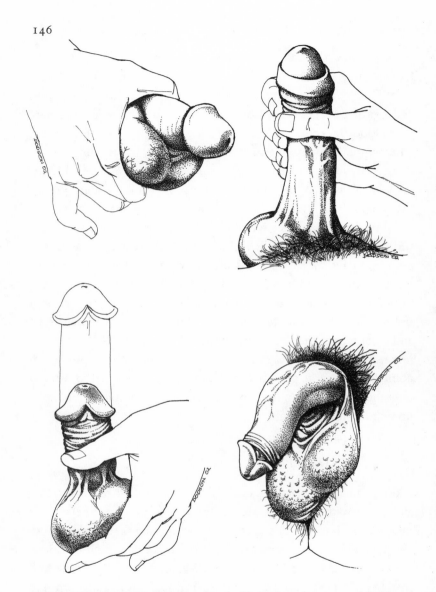

PENIS VARIATIONS. *Many penises double in size when erect, while big penises grow less in length and girth. Around the turn of the twentieth century, society changed the focus of what represented virile manhood from the size of the testicles to the size of the penis. This shift has created a lot of insecurity in many men who feel sexually inadequate although they have healthy average-sized penises.*

Eric is part of generation-X, which takes condoms for granted. When he became sexually active, he discovered that at first, when condoms are nice and tight, they dampen sexual sensation, which aids control. However, during intercourse, the condom stretches, even with plenty of lubricant. The sensual feeling of the vagina along with a loose condom rubbing over his dickhead created additional stimulation, and this combination caused him to come too quickly many a time. Convinced partnersex could be better, he set out to develop what he calls "come control." Along with reading every book he could find on sex, he masturbated with no concern about going blind.

Conscious Masturbation. If you are not circumcised, your own foreskin will give you plenty of lubrication and sensation. If you are circumcised, a quality massage oil will make masturbation far more sensual. If none is available, use a combination of saliva and precome. There are many ways to handle your penis. Some men use the palm of their hand circling the shaft and others circle the glans or head of the dick with a thumb and forefinger. A few use both hands. One right-handed friend referred to his right hand as his wife, while his left hand was his mistress.

Experiment by trying different techniques. It's a good idea to vary the rhythm and use a light grip. Your other hand can massage any part of your body that feels good—your testicles, nipples, or anus. Pay attention to the sensations—what feels good, what feels neutral, and what gets your buildup going. Conscious masturbation will allow you to get more familiar with your entire arousal process. Try to practice several times a week like an athlete working out or a musician learning to play an instrument.

It took Eric a year to gain fairly consistent control during masturbation. At the end of two years, he was confident he could last at least thirty minutes and sometimes longer with a partner. By the time we met, he was so sexually proficient that against all odds, he convinced me to let him move in with me. I often tease him by saying his sexual abilities allowed him to fuck his way out of the upper-middle-class ghetto of the south and move into the heart of New York City with a sugar mama.

The Classic Squeeze Technique. This is what most books and magazines discuss. Masters and Johnson recommended this method for married couples, with the wife providing manual stimulation for her husband. While she masturbated him, he would tell her when he was getting close to coming. Then she would stop and pinch just under the glans of his penis until the urge to ejaculate subsided. After a few moments, she resumed manual stimulation, repeating the process. Some men complained their wives were too rough when they pinched them, so I suspect a few were expressing old resentments. Besides, why should it be her job when it's his dick?

My recommendation is for each man to train himself long before he gets married. However, if you are currently married, it's never too late to improve if you're willing to put in a little time practicing—the same way you would out on the driving range. If you're married, create a space where you can have some privacy, even if it's in the basement. While masturbating, just before feeling the surge toward ejaculation, stop and press your thumb and finger just under the rim of the glans or head of the penis and/or at the base. The semen travels through the urethral tube that runs up the underside of the penis. Squeezing this tube and relaxing helps to retard ejaculation. After chilling out a moment, start stroking again. Repeating this process will allow you to experience and sustain higher levels of sexual arousal.

Some men think about something not related to sex in their effort to impede a climax. Eric said he learned to become a "fuck monk," as he calls it, putting all sexual images or hot fantasies out of his mind. Instead, he focused on tender feelings of benevolence toward an imaginary girlfriend while playing somber or sweet music to help the process. After much solo work, he did the same thing later with a partner and experienced his first breakthrough with ejaculatory control during intercourse when he was in college.

Stop/Start. While masturbating, instead of squeezing, simply stop all stimulation just before the autonomic ejaculation system kicks in by taking your hand away. As your dick stands alone in the breeze, you might feel a tight sensation or a slight cramping, but nothing painful. Once the orgasmic feeling calms down you can start stroking again. Within a short period of time, mild orgasmic feelings leading up to ejaculation will return. Again, take your hand away before the autonomic ejaculation switch is thrown. One friend of mine called this process "staying on rainbow ridge."

One time when Eric was using this technique and stopped, he saw his dickhead swell slightly of its own accord. Droplets of watery ejaculate emerged from the tip. His load was suspended at the tip of his cock. He was very excited knowing he could stop the freight train almost on a dime. He then used his thumb and forefinger to massage the semen back down toward the perineum, pressing along the urethra on the underside of his shaft. Now he can go up as many times as he wants, taking as much time as desired while savoring the mild orgasmic feelings by simply taking his hand away during self-love, or stopping his stroke deep inside a partner.

Enjoying orgasmic sensations without the finality of ejaculation is pleasurable. As great as it feels, Eric doesn't consider himself to be multiorgasmic then or now. He is enjoying the preorgasmic sensations just before ejaculation. He isn't shooting and then moving on to another orgasm without losing his hardon, and he isn't having a full-blown orgasm without ejaculation. When the spirit moves him he keeps the stimulation going and comes. Sometimes the resulting orgasm is more powerful, and at other times it feels diminished. It's as though he has broken down his orgasm into smaller pieces, enjoying the parts individually. This technique has extended his "hard time."

PELVIC FLOOR MUSCLES

The PC, or pubococcygeal, muscle is a key player in sexual pleasure. It affects a man's ability to get hard, stay hard, and have a full orgasm. This is the muscle that contracts involuntarily during ejaculation. To locate the muscle, stop the flow of urine. Men need to strengthen their PC muscle by consciously squeezing and releasing it during rounds of repetitions. As you grow older, weak pelvic floor muscles will result in urinary incontinence, difficulty in getting erect, and weaker ejaculations with orgasm.

Women often struggle to have orgasms, so I suggest they pump the PC muscle. Men often struggle to keep from coming, so relaxing the PC muscle helps. Other men claim that tightening the PC helps to hold off orgasm. Some bear down a bit, which is done with the same muscular movement as that used to force the stream of urine to flow faster. While masturbating, observe your PC muscle during moments that feel most pleasurable and experiment to see what works best. Use any technique that will keep you from coming too quickly. Just remember that keeping the PC muscle relaxed is a constant challenge. Eric tells me how even after years of conscious control, it's easy to get caught up in the sex and suddenly realize he's climbing to orgasm because his PC has unconsciously tightened. Taking slow, deep belly breaths will help to relax the muscle.

Some men learn to orgasm without ejaculating at all, but this has always sounded a bit too puritanical to me. In my opinion, semen savers are like sexual misers. It would be like saving saliva because you think you have a limited amount. I think few American men would be interested in taking the time to learn these involved Eastern techniques, which take years of practice to master. However, for any man who is interested, there are many books on Tao and Tantra sex that explain the process. Not ejaculating also contradicts the idea that having consistent ejaculations is a way to maintain prostate gland health and avoid problems later on.

Devoting all of your JO time to disciplined introspection would become a drag, so you must allow yourself sessions for pleasure only, some for practice only, and at times try a combination of the two. In either case, always treat yourself to an orgasm in the end. Another helpful exercise is conscious masturbation with porn videos. Play a game to see if you can last longer than the guy in the video. What makes watching porn and masturbating so effective is that you not only have cock stimulation with your hand, you also have the visual and auditory erotic input, which is much closer to the reality of having sex with a partner.

KISSING

Your mouth, lips, and tongue are major providers of sexual pleasure. Having a partner who is a good kisser usually means a lot to most women. For me it's a general indication of how sensuous a man will be. There is definitely an art to kissing, usually with a relaxed mouth and tender touches at first, then graduating to wet tongue kissing that is more leisurely done than what we often see in the movies. The technique to avoid is what I call "mouth mauling," where a couple appears to be devouring each other's lips and tongues like cannibals. Sloppier, wetter, and deeper tongue kissing does not make it more passionate—quite the opposite. Instead of trying to outdo each other, agree to take turns: take the lead and pleasure your partner's mouth with your lips and tongue while she receives. Then hold still and let her do the same to you.

Eric and I enjoy sharing chocolate kisses. We keep a container of chocolate ice cream in the freezer. Occasionally he will fill his mouth with a spoonful and as we kiss, I lick and suck to get as much as I can while he allows a little bit at a time to enter my mouth. When I get a chunk of chocolate, instead of swallowing it I'll push it back into his mouth with my tongue, and until it melts, we go back and forth. A chocolate kiss can last for several minutes and they are always delightful.

TOUCHING

There's nothing better than a man who takes care of his hands. Many women—like myself—are as attracted to a man's hands as much as they are to his face, body, or penis. Being aware of how we touch someone else's body is a cornerstone of pleasurable sex. Those of us who came from affectionate homes usually feel more comfortable about touching and being touched. Others are touch-starved and can feel awkward or uncomfortable while being hugged or caressed. Some are extremely ticklish or "touchy" and pull away or are constantly complaining about something hurting.

If you are with a woman who has never touched her own sex organs or breasts, being gentle is a must. It's similar to guys who are very "touchy" about their testicles because they never handle them and end up cringing from a gentle caress. When it comes to touching a woman's vulva, make sure your fingernails are clean, smooth, and short. If work keeps your hands rough, wearing a tight-fitting latex glove like the ones your dentist wears will solve the problem. Pay attention to your hands because they are primary instruments of pleasure for yourself and your lover.

Remember The Pointer Sisters singing "I want a man with a slow hand"? Most women would agree, so slow down and lighten up with all forms of pussy petting and clitoral touching. Before contacting the delicate mucous membrane of her genitals, cover your fingers with massage oil. If there is none available at least use saliva until you can dip a finger just inside her vagina and use her own lubrication. But don't rely on her being wet. She might be nervous or tense. It's a good idea to keep a bottle of massage oil next to the bed. If you're going to her place, take some massage oil, condoms, and a water-based lube. Use the oil for genital massage at first, but after the condom goes on, use a water-based lube to keep the latex from breaking down.

After making sure she's comfortable physically and emotionally, easing your way in through the intricate folds of her labia is a slow process that requires a gentle touch. Once in between the outer and inner lips, instead of putting pressure directly on her clit in one place, try stroking the general area, making occasional passes over the clitoris to warm her up gradually. After several minutes you can begin to use a more direct form of clitoral contact, always varying the rhythm and keeping it light and wet. A workshop woman complained that her husband rubbed her clitoris so hard it felt as if he was trying to erase it. Just as sad was her inability to open her mouth and tell him what she wanted.

The best way to discover the kind of clitoral touching your girlfriend prefers is to ask her to show you the amount of pressure she wants by using her fingers on the back of your hand. It's even better to try out different strokes on her vulva while getting verbal feedback on what feels best to her while you're having partnersex. If she complains that you're being "too clinical," be patient and tell her how much it means to you to please her. This kind of sharing can go both ways between couples so they can learn about each other's preferences for manual sex.

ORALSEX

After years of listening to women, many first-time orgasms with a lover have been the result of oralsex. For some reason the French are credited with having invented oralsex. Some American men don't think oralsex qualifies as real sex, especially married men. But believe me, for the woman doing the cocksucking, it's more than real. Most of these guys are referring to *getting* a blowjob without returning the favor by going down on a woman. Men who do this are either paying for sex, or they're in a position of power and she's using sex as a bargaining chip. Let me assure you that oralsex is undoubtedly one of the most intimate things a man and woman can share.

If you are totally hooked on "tits and ass" and know nothing about vulvas, I suggest you stop wanking to centerfold nudes and start getting some good cunt photography. Check out the Genital Art Forum on my website as well as X-rated videos and girlie magazines to discover the enormous varieties of female genitals so you can tune into the beauty of the different forms. Also, you won't spontaneously turn gay by checking out the variety of male genitals as well.

If you are already a connoisseur of cunts and you love the form of her genitals, but discover her pussy doesn't smell good to you, suggest taking a shower together. It's fun to sensuously lather up each other's genitals while getting turned on at the same time. We all have our own unique scent and flavor. Our diets and personal hygiene are a central factor. The same is true for men's semen. Pussy juice and jism are acquired tastes, like drinking martinis or eating expensive, aged French cheeses.

The standard hang-ups for women when it comes to receiving oralsex are still basically the same as I had. I was afraid my genitals were ugly, they wouldn't taste good, and it would take me too long to have an orgasm. When you first go down on her, compliment her on how pretty her pussy is, and after several licks, tell her how sweet she tastes. Let her know that you enjoy what you're doing. Make sure you are comfortable. There's nothing worse for a woman than seeing her boyfriend in an uncomfortable position before he even starts giving head. If you can honestly project the feeling that you want to be there for as long as she will allow it, it's very reassuring. If you can't, then don't try faking it. That never works; women's radar picks it up.

Keep things delicate, soft, and wet. Vary the rhythm and pressure by flexing your tongue and flattening it to lap at a larger area. Occasionally probe her vaginal opening with an erect tongue. Pucker up and circle your wet lips over and over around her clit. Once you're sure she's lubricated, slowly inch your way into her vagina with your finger while you continue tonguing her clitoris. When you feel her vagina relax and melt into liquid silk, use both fingers. Either hold your hand still or move it slowly back and forth. Alternate oralsex with your hand to give your tongue and jaw a rest.

Instead of looking for her special G-spot and digging at it with rapid in and out friction like a jackhammer, just press your fingers up toward the ceiling of her vagina and make wavelike motions while you stay with her clitty. Women are faking guys out right and left with this business of female ejaculation. Don't use the volume or the repeated number of her squirts as a sign that you've made her come really hard. A lot of women can shoot diluted urine that doesn't taste or smell like urine and they're not sexually aroused at all. If golden showers turn both of you on, then that's great. Go for it.

On her final approach to orgasm, there's a natural tendency to get excited and intensify whatever it is you're doing. Speeding up or changing the stimulation usually throws a woman off track. Keep things steady and consistent all the way through to orgasm. Both women and men can be uncomfortably hypersensitive just after an orgasm. As her come subsides, lighten your touch for a few moments but stay with her. She might want to keep going and have another climax.

SLOW PENETRATION

This is one of the most neglected of all sexual skills. Plunging thoughtlessly inside a vagina is the result of sexual repression and deprivation. A friend of mine admitted that when he got close to a vaginal opening, he feared that if he didn't get his penis inside fast, the woman would change her mind and the whole deal would be off. Another fear is losing an erection. Some men feel they have to penetrate fast before their penis goes soft. How many movies have we seen where the hero mounts a woman and within seconds he's in full thrusting mode.

It's important to warm every woman up with clitoral stimulation before entering her vagina. To see if she's ready, place the pad of your finger at her vaginal opening. Apply just a slight bit of pres-

sure to feel if she's moist or wet. If she feels dry, add more lubrication and continue with small circles or light stroking going back to
her clitoris while occasionally dipping down toward the vaginal
opening. As you feel her vaginal muscle relaxing, press inside slowly.
Go just an inch at a time, feeling the soft folds of her vagina making room for your finger. When you are inside, hold still a moment
so she can fully relax. Then slowly circle your finger or make wavelike motions. After a few moments, pull your finger out and go back
to her clitoris.

Choose a position that will allow you or her to continue clitoral stimulation while you're fucking. With your cock poised at
her vaginal opening, enter her vagina with your penis the same as
with your finger, bit by bit. Once again, be a tease by holding back
and making her want more of you inside. Most of her penetration
sensation is at the opening of the vagina. If she's getting the combination of clitoral stimulation during penetration, she'll feel more
if you go slowly while both of you use your PC muscles to enhance
every stroke.

No one style of clitoral touch will work for all women. Again,
it will be your ability to discuss this with each girlfriend to find out
what she likes that will make you a memorable lover. If you're dating a woman who says, "Oh, everything you do is wonderful," don't
believe her for one minute. She is trying to make you think you
are God's gift to womankind to get you to fall in love with her. Get
smart and don't buy into this kind of false flattery.

Penetrating a pussy is a major initiation ritual to qualify as a
man, but it's seldom done sensuously enough to create any pleasure for a young woman. The pain and disappointment of first-time
partnersex is so common that it's chalked up as an unfortunate
inevitability of womanhood. Is it any wonder why so many young
women don't look forward to having intercourse again? A similar
problem exists for young men. If first-time partnersex ends with
premature ejaculation, or he can't penetrate her because of her
hymen, he can feel humiliated.

Many young girls lose their virginity when they learn to use a tampon. One client told me she had a very tough hymen that needed to be opened surgically. Women like myself, who were physically active and sexually curious, have no memory of having to stretch our hymens because it happened so gradually. The best approach would be for a young woman to be the first person to penetrate her own vagina.

Eric has been with quite a few women experiencing penetration sex for the first time. He begins by spending at least ten minutes leisurely stroking the woman's entire vulva using massage oil. This lets her know his touch will be gentle and she can relax a bit more. His hands pass over her clitoris—without focusing on it—with the intention of getting her hot. Instead, he lets her sexual desire build slowly. Once he feels she trusts him and is getting comfortable, he shifts over to oralsex. While rolling his tongue over her clitoris, he slowly eases one finger inside her now moist vagina. Adding a second finger helps to prepare her for the girth of a penis. If she has an orgasm with oralsex, this makes penetration with his penis even easier.

Depending upon the woman, he uses a position that allows her to have clitoral stimulation during penetration provided by either him or her. If she feels comfortable with the idea, it's effective for a penetration virgin to control the entire process by getting on top. After putting on a condom, he applies some water-based lube to his dick and her vagina. He starts with shallow penetration using just the head of his penis. While pushing in very slightly, he encourages her to squeeze and release her vaginal muscle. This helps her to relax the muscle and allows him to move inside little by little with minimal discomfort. When first-time partnersex is pleasurable (without any concern of STDs or pregnancy) women invariably want more.

For every Sleeping Beauty created through female repression there is a sexually uninformed Prince Charming under a lot of pressure to awaken her. A man's conditioning to give a woman an orgasm is the counterpart to a woman's conditioning to be passive. When you base your self-esteem on being the only legitimate source of her sexual pleasure, you unknowingly set up one of the biggest barriers to becoming a world-class lover. Encouraging your girlfriend or wife to be part of the sexual dance by taking control of her own clitoral stimulation is the biggest step any man can take toward creating sexual equality.

For those of us who like sex, there's nothing better than a skilled lover. However, all kinds of physical touching—like affectionate hugging and kissing—are every bit as important as having an orgasm to most women. Also, don't hold back on dishing out lots of sweet talk and showing her how much you care for her every day. Each woman's positive response will more than compensate any man who does this. Remember, what goes around comes around, especially when it comes to sharing orgasmic partnersex.

✴ 12 ✴

I'LL SHOW YOU MINE

Our Magnificent Sex Organs

T HROUGHOUT HISTORY, the human genitals have been
feared, worshiped, mutilated, ignored, and admired. There
are many historical examples of male phalluses and female
vulvas being honored as symbols of fertility. Pre-Columbian statues showed a baby's head emerging from a vagina. Huge penises
still stand in Japanese temples. Ancient India held both male and
female sex organs in high esteem and sexuality was seen as a spiritual practice in the Tantra religion. Older cultures based on goddess worship and pagan rituals that were not part of recorded
history also revered the human sex organs. The nude body and genitals of both women and men have been the subject of art from as
far back as the Stone Age. However, none of these relics depicted
the clitoris—none.

In ancient Greece, artists carved exquisite male statues with penises, but when it came to women's genitals, they were represented with a triangular shape or draped with a cloth. During the Italian Renaissance, artists painted sensuous nudes using religious themes from the Bible. One of the later popes had all of Michelangelo's male genitals covered with leaves or loincloths, and many Greek statues had their genitals broken off. As Christianity continued to denounce all bodily pleasures, the human sex organs became a source of shame, from which many of us still suffer to this day.

In spite of organized religion's efforts to control people and their sexual urges, we now have a billion-dollar adult industry pumping out images of women and men's genitals in videos and magazines. From the early eight-millimeter stag movies to the sixties split beaver magazines, there was always a variety of genital styles and body types. Today, the adult industry's standard image of sexual desirability favors a thin female body with big tits, long legs, and neatly shaved pussies with small inner lips. Women are getting breast implants and snipping off those lovely long butterfly labia to conform to this current ideal. Most of the male actors have muscular bodies and large dicks. The sex industry is no different from the advertising and fashion industries which present a stereotype of beauty that few of us can attain.

MINE

When I first looked at my sex organ with a mirror, I must have been around ten years old. Without a name or any images for the inner labia, I was horrified when I saw two awful dangling chicken wattles that didn't even match. The one on the right side was a lot longer than the one on the left. Clearly I'd stretched them from playing with myself too much. Rather than give up this solitary pleasure, from that day on I started masturbating with my finger on the left side to see if I could even them up, but they stayed the same.

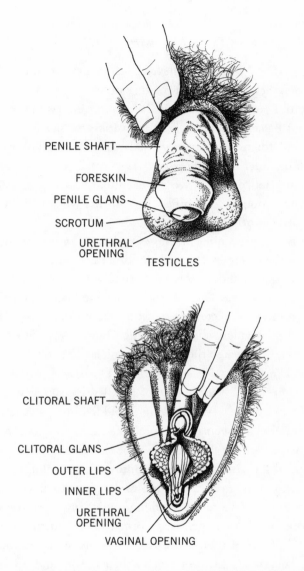

PENILE SHAFT

FORESKIN

PENILE GLANS

SCROTUM

URETHRAL
OPENING

TESTICLES

CLITORAL SHAFT

CLITORAL GLANS

OUTER LIPS

INNER LIPS

URETHRAL
OPENING

VAGINAL OPENING

THE EXTERNAL MALE AND FEMALE GENITALIA. *Here we see
the similarities between the outer parts of the male and female sex organs.
The external genitals of both sexes arise at a common site and during the
first seven weeks of life they are undifferentiated. The clitoral glans enlarges
to become the glans penis. The shaft of the clitoris elongates to become the
shaft of the penis. The outer lips turn into the male scrotum. Viva la
similarities as well as the differences.*

Until I was thirty-five, I honestly believed I was genitally deformed from the innocent act of childhood masturbation.

It wasn't until I saw pictures of other women's genitals in girlie magazines that I began to realize the huge variety of shapes, colors, textures, and forms of female genitals that included short, medium, and long inner lips. My sex life was so totally transformed by that one experience that I would eventually create genital imagery and teach thousands of other women that we are all different and beautiful works of art.

After setting up an evening of photographing a group of my friends' vulvas in the seventies, I traveled around the country with a carousel of female genital slides, showing them to women and mixed groups at colleges as well as feminist gatherings. Audiences everywhere would become completely silent with their mouths hanging open while I talked lovingly about Valentine Cunts. Showing one slide after another, I compared the different genital styles to periods of architecture like Gothic, Renaissance, Art Deco, and Swedish Modern. Although I acted very matter-of-fact, I was shaking with fear inside, fully aware that I was showing forbidden images. A few people present might have seen a photo or looked at a woman's genitals, but most were viewing this image for the first time.

After I stopped showing the slides, I continued to sit alongside countless women pointing out the exquisite design of their vulvas in my Bodysex groups. As a result of taking one of my workshops and feeling good about their genitals, women have told me that they put a small photo of their vulva in a locket to wear around their necks. Others have taken portraits of their pussies and made them into valentines for a lover. A few women reclaimed their genitals by wearing gold or silver rings in one or both inner lips. I had a portrait of my cunt carved into a jade pendent that I wore on a silver chain around my neck for years. In the nineties, to celebrate twenty-five years of female genital appreciation, I produced the videotape *Viva la Vulva,* which shows a group of ten women trimming and shaving their pubic hair in preparation for pussy portraits.

Since I began my cunt crusade in the seventies, an abundance of genital art and images have appeared. Yet each new generation of women start out with genital shame. To get beyond the procreation image of heterosexuality and factor in genital pride and sexual pleasure, mothers have to stop telling their children that boys have a penis and girls have a vagina. Instead, our children need to be told that boys have a penis and girls have a clitoris. When a boy touches his penis or a girl touches her clitoris in a special way, both of them will feel nice tingly sensations. Later, when children get a bit older, they also need to be told that a boy's penis will ejaculate white semen and a girl's vagina will pass red blood—*before* it actually happens. It isn't fair that many children end up traumatized by these totally natural occurrences that should be cause for celebration.

In 1981 a group of women self-helpers in L.A. finally gave us a description of the entire clitoris in *A New View of a Woman's Body*. Ten women who were part of the Federation of Feminist Women's Health Centers conducted the research. Originally published by Simon & Schuster, the book seemed to vanish after a year. Many years later, the book reappeared, and this time it was distributed by the Women's Health Centers themselves. Rebecca Chalker, a member of the original collective, is now part of my women's sexual study group. We are all in the field of sex and meet every month to discuss a variety of topics and share sex information. Rebecca's latest book is titled *The Clitoral Truth*.

In every workshop I ran, I always pointed out the shaft, glans, and hood of the clitoris, presenting a limited view. Thanks to the illustrations in *A New View*, I finally understood what defines the clitoris in its entirety. That tiny little pearl peeking out from under the hood is not the whole story. The internal structure of the clitoris is made up of the legs, bulbs, and urethral sponge. These interior parts are erectile tissue that becomes engorged with blood during sexual arousal—the same process that causes a penis to become erect. Without this basic knowledge, its no wonder so many women believe their sex organ is their vagina. A woman's erectile tissue occupies nearly the same amount of space as a man's, except most of ours are inside our bodies.

The shaft of the clitoris divides into two parts that spread out like a wishbone called the crura, or the legs of the clitoris. These two anchoring wingtips of erectile tissue are about three inches long. Starting from where the shaft and the legs meet, and continuing down underneath the inner lips, there are two bundles of erectile tissue called the bulbs of the clitoris. The whole clitoris is the glans, hood, shaft, legs, and vestibular bulbs—these organs are there solely for sexual pleasure. In *A New View,* the women include the inner lips, the urethral sponge, and the perineal sponge as parts of the clitoris because they engorge during sexual arousal, contributing to women's sexual pleasure.

It's not just the poor and uneducated who are sexually ignorant. A letter from a forty-seven-year-old Ph.D. school psychologist said she is from a repressed family of four sisters. They had all spent most of their energies being "A" students in life's endeavors. Unfortunately, she has to give all four of them a D– for knowledge and appreciation of themselves. In the past four months, she finally discovered that rubbing her clitoris feels good! Although she is "developmentally delayed sexually" she is defiantly enjoying these new discoveries, both with herself and her husband. She sent one of her sisters a copy of my book and a small battery-operated vibrator for her birthday to begin a new era for her family of women.

Another letter, this one from a twenty-one-year-old college student who performed in *The Vagina Monologues* at school, said that after having sex with three different men who failed to give her an orgasm, she didn't know where to start. She was sorry to hear I no longer ran "vagina workshops." That's been my criticism about the *Monologues* all along—the play doesn't sexually inform women but rather perpetuates the myth that the vagina is a woman's sex organ. No wonder women continue to think they should be able to have an orgasm from intercourse alone.

The first time I saw *The Vagina Monologues* was off–Broadway, where I heard a charming young woman named Eve Ensler talk about my work with a distorted view of what I'd been doing for twenty-five years. She called it "The Vagina Workshop" and said there was actually a woman who ran these groups. She described the workshops' participants looking at their "vaginas" with a hand mirror trying to find their "G-spots." The entire monologue grossly misrepresented my workshops. Although Eve is a playwright and entitled to use poetic license, I had to confront her about not mentioning the word "clitoris" in describing my groups. As a matter of fact, the word "clitoris" was never mentioned during her entire original play. Later, in her dressing room, I said my workshops had been carefully designed to help women find the real source of their sexual stimulation—the clitoris. To her credit, Ensler later added "clitoris."

In February 1998, *The Vagina Monologues* joined forces with the Ms. Foundation with a benefit performance celebrating V-Day. By February 2001, they had corporate sponsorship and filled Madison Square Garden for another fund-raiser. The women reading the monologues were culled from the biggest names in screen and television. Both nights made it clear that the format of the original play had dramatically changed. We were brought to a delirious high during the first half only to be plunged down, drowning in a sea filled with the horrors of violence against women. We were told about the vast numbers of women being raped, tortured, and genitally mutilated in Africa, Bosnia, and Afghanistan. *V* no longer stood for vagina, it stood for violence.

Sex and violence, never sex and pleasure. Talking about sexual pleasure would be too frivolous, inappropriate, and politically incorrect. And who is to blame for all the sexual violence against women? According to V-Day feminists it is still the patriarchy. Does that mean daddy, our brothers, and our husbands? Is it the pope or God? Dare I be so bold as to say the source of violence against

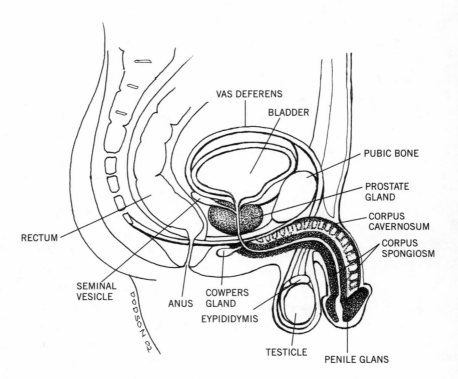

CROSS SECTION OF THE MALE GENITALS. *Although it is usually assumed that men have a far greater volume of erectile tissue than women, who have only a small, pea-like clit, when we compare the amount of erectile tissue in men and women it is actually similar. The shaded areas show the erectile tissue of the penis: The penile glans, the (corps) corpus cavernosum, and the corpus spongeosum. The prostate gland also swells during sexual excitement. The testicles are where the sperm cells are manufactured. When the sperm matures, it passes from the testicle to the epididimis and into the vas deferens. On the way to ejaculation, the sperm are mixed with fluids from the seminal vesicles, prostate gland, and Cowper's gland to create semen. This mixture protects the billions of sperm as they travel inside a naturally acidic vagina heading for the fertile egg.*

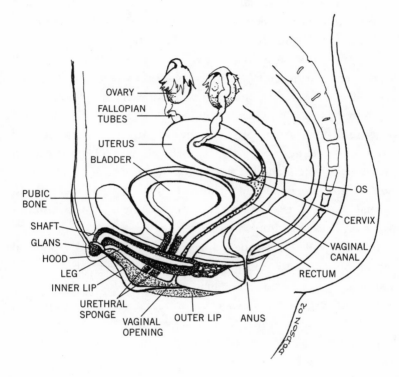

OVARY

FALLOPIAN TUBES

UTERUS

BLADDER

PUBIC BONE

SHAFT

GLANS

HOOD

LEG

INNER LIP

URETHRAL SPONGE

VAGINAL OPENING

OUTER LIP

ANUS

OS

CERVIX

VAGINAL CANAL

RECTUM

CROSS SECTION OF THE FEMALE GENITALS. *The shaded areas show the erectile tissue in the female: The glans of the clitoris and the clitoral shaft, the legs of the clitoris, the vestibular bulb, and the urethral and perineal sponges all become engorged during sexual arousal. The inner and outer lips become fuller and deepen in color with sexual excitement. The eggs are matured in the ovaries. In the middle of a woman's menstrual cycle, an egg travels down the fallopian tube into the uterus, waiting to be fertilized by a sperm cell for up to four days. Unless pregnancy occurs, the uterus bleeds out the lining (endometrium) every month to repeat the cycle again until a woman reaches menopause.*

women comes from fundamentalists in all the major religions—
Christians, Jews, Hindus, and Muslims?

After writing a critical review of the *Monologues*, which had
become another sacred cow, I was told by one of the organizers
that I suffered from the "Queen Bee Syndrome." One writer
accused me of being jealous of Eve's success. It's my belief that all
art is open to criticism in a democracy. It's no secret that I'm pissed
off at all the matriarchal feminists who are every bit as authoritarian as any patriarchy when it comes to women embracing sexual
pleasure. The original play was humorous and charming and
women left feeling happy to be women, but the V-Day version had
me agreeing with Camille Paglia when she wrote: "With her obsession with male evil and her claimed history of physical abuse and
mental breakdowns, Ensler is the new Andrea Dworkin, minus
Medusan hair and rumpled farm overalls."

My friend Penny Arcade is a performance artist with a political
awareness similar to George Carlin's. At one point she tells her
audience, "I hope you're not here to see *The Vagina Monologues*,
because my vagina does not speak, nor does it have a favorite color,
nor does it wear a funny hat." She says younger women howl with
laughter, but the older set doesn't see that the sexual content of the
Monologues is just so much fluff.

Right here at home, everyone gets a piece of our pussies, but
they rarely belong to the woman herself. First, our genitals belong
to our mothers, who bathe us and change our diapers when we are
infants. Then they are controlled by whatever religion is practiced
in the home, usually with a mild or strong message about not
touching ourselves "down there." Next we fall into romantic love
and our first boyfriend explores our genitals before we even know
anything about the form or function of our own sex organ. Later,
we give them to the man we marry and finally hand them over to
a gynecologist/obstetrician, where the cycle starts all over again for
the next generation of women.

Here's an example of a woman from the Genital Art Forum on my website who has claimed her own sex organ:

> I prefer the word "cunt" because it sounds strong, even a little fierce. It's like that ancient Celtic female symbol often carved of stone showing a woman spreading her labia wide enough to take in the whole world. That's how I feel when my clit gets a hardon. I can actually grab it with the tips of my fingers and move it up and down like a tiny penis. I feel more affectionate toward my labia these days. When they puff up they look like stage curtains drawing apart to present the opening act of the evening: "Please welcome Miss-s-s-s Clitty!" In my youth I was obsessed with the fact that my long labia never resembled any of those uniform airbrushed slits I'd seen in men's magazines. Where were their inner lips? Did they tuck them inside? Eventually I saw more images of cunts that revealed an amazing diversity. They are as different from one another as an iris is from a rose from an orchid.

YOURS

Far too many men are overly concerned with the size of their dicks instead of focusing on mastering sexual skills to become great lovers. Although it has been said, "It's not the size of the fish but the motion of the ocean," I believe penis size matters to a degree. For those women and men who prefer a large penis, there's no reason to make them feel badly about their sexual preference. However, according to the thousands of women I've talked with, most of them are more interested in what surrounds the penis—the whole man. Getting fucked by a giant, rock-hard cock that shoots a huge load of semen is a man's fantasy of male sexual prowess, not a woman's.

While some experts claim a vagina is a collapsed space that will accommodate any size penis, I disagree. My own vaginal barrel is around six inches deep, so I have a problem if a man's penis is too big. Then I know it can hurt and I'm unable to relax and move freely. Small doesn't matter that much because even a finger inside my vagina feels good with the right rhythm and movement. Besides, like most women, I can't come from penis/vagina sex, so I'm more interested in what's happening to my clit.

Some penises I have enjoyed with clit stim over the years are: a five-and-one-half inch, curved, lavender-colored, uncut cock; a big, thick, black dick that was a whopping nine inches, which meant I had to negotiate the last couple of inches; a five-inch, short but very fat, circumcised Jewish dick; a nice six-and-a-half-inch Dutch dick with an enormous vein running down the shaft; and Eric's seven-inch peter that currently has me "dick addicted." He actually thought his penis was on the small size from watching porn, but it's a bit too big to do deep penetration unless I'm in a high state of arousal. Men need to stop comparing their dick size to those of porn actors who are chosen almost solely because they have huge cocks. And who is choosing those large dicks? Other men, of course. My friend Richard Pacheco is the only porn star I know of with an average-size penis, and he has retired from the business.

Not long ago I went to a website that promised to increase the size of a man's penis, but never said how to other than through some form of exercise. Listen to your aunt Betty. I wasn't about to pay for their information; besides, I already knew the exercise would most likely be regular masturbation. As yet, science has not developed a successful way to enlarge a penis. The vacuum pumps will increase penis size temporarily. Similar to masturbation, pumping up your dick is an exercise that expands the corpus cavernosum and spongiosum so they can take in more blood, which is what causes an erection. It's the "use it or lose it" principle.

The best way to exercise your penis is to masturbate to orgasm frequently. Be sure to use massage oil, especially if you are circumcised. In the process, you can also train yourself to have come control, which is more important to women than dick size. Men also need to tune into their pelvic floor muscle. A friend of mine who acted in porn showed me the strength of his PC muscle. When I put my finger inside his buttyhole it was caught in a viselike grip. He explained most guys in porn develop a strong PC muscle to help them get it up and keep it up. Every time you masturbate to orgasm, you are pumping blood into your penis and using the surrounding muscles.

Penis worship is alive and well in the gay men's community, but heterosexual men also worship penis size. They just don't do it openly. They tease each other about having small dicks and that generates a lot of unnecessary sexual insecurity in men who are already uneasy about sexuality. Here is an example from a twenty-three-year-old man:

> My penis is just five inches long. I have never had intercourse. I would like to try it but I'm worried about the length of my penis. I'm afraid the girl will complain that it is too short since my friends tell me it is. Sometime I feel embarrassed showing my penis when I get naked in the gym to shower. Betty, is it important to have a long penis? Is my penis length normal? Does every girl and woman out there prefer a long penis and is there any way I can make mine longer?

The average-size penis is said to be between five and a half and six inches. So according to statistics, he's short by only half an inch. But he might have a five-inch fat sausage that many women would love. Due to popular request, sex shops started stocking short, fat dildos for their women clients. Instead of worrying about penis size, he would do well to educate himself about female sexuality. The biggest dick in the world will not stimulate a woman's clitoris. When I hear from a man who has an even smaller penis (in the three- to four-inch category erect) I advise him to pretend his tongue has taken up jogging and get a reputation for giving great head instead of feeling sorry for himself. He can become a world-class cunt sucker who will have women standing in line waiting to be next.

The Kama Sutra and Native Americans compared both male and female genitals to different animals: deer, elephant, horse, dog, etc. A small dog dick in an elephant vagina would be lost in space. Perhaps in a more sexually sophisticated society, women and men would have a chance to compare genital sizes like they try on shoes. I've always suspected the fairy tale of Cinderella with the prince running around looking for a foot to fit a shoe was symbolism for finding a vagina to fit his dick.

The comedian George Carlin got it right when he talked about why Americans consistently declare war and bomb "brown peo-ple." It's based on "dick fear." He then goes on to talk about how the whole missile program is the result of dick fear. Americans have to make sure they have the biggest dicks with the biggest bang for the buck. We laugh at this, but I have long believed that fewer men would need to shoot missiles and guns if they could shoot a little come from their hard cocks for fun. There's an old saying in the army that the only difference between a man's rifle and his penis is that one is for fighting and the other is for fun. But how many men are actually having fun with their penises?

The sensitive parts on most men's penises are the rim of the glans and the little V-shaped area underneath the glans that I call the male clitoris. The urethral opening also has sensitivity. I've known men who have enjoyed a stream of water hitting their lit-tle pee hole in the shower to get turned on. One friend of mine actually inserts a sterilized and lubricated rod inside his urethra because he enjoys the sensation, and an older friend uses surgically wrapped thin plastic tubes to keep his urinary tract open. His doc-tor taught him how to do it.

Some men like to have their prostate gland massaged with a fin-ger during oral or manual sex but prostate massage is rarely an end in itself. Most guys still want the head and shaft of their dick involved in order to blow out a great orgasm. When your girlfriend is adding prostate stimulation with a finger inside your anus to heighten manual or oral sex, tell her what feels best. Having her relying on your feedback is better than having her look for a specific place like your P-spot, which can be intimidating.

All the different male animals, including humans, have a built-in drive to copulate. Depending upon your point of view, God, Mother Nature, or human evolution set it up like this to ensure the continuation of our species. This desire, obsession, or force driving you to come inside a pussy is how men have been hardwired. So relax. You are not a sex fiend because you think about sex every few minutes or so. You are just a healthy guy pumping a lot of testosterone trying to fulfill your biological purpose—procreation. As long as you can get it up, put it in, and ejaculate you have made God, Mother Nature, or human evolution happy. However, the woman you get pregnant will either be delighted or furious with you.

Women's hardwiring tells us to get some kind of commitment before we let you put it in—an engagement ring or better yet, a marriage contract. You just want to come but we have the burden of caring for a child throughout the prime of our lifetime and sometimes later as grandmothers. My advice to all single men is to masturbate right before you go out to take the edge off that raging bull between your legs. If she wants to have sex with you, masturbating earlier in the evening will help you last longer.

Honoring both the male and female phalluses equally would begin to heal a world out of balance. We spend trillions of dollars going into outer space, yet we spend very little exploring the inner space of our own sexual anatomy. Americans could easily provide an adequate sex education for our children that would include information about the magnificent male and female phalluses—his penis and her clitoris. We could replace the shame most adults feel about their genitals with the acceptance and wonder I remember having as a child when we innocently played "I'll show you mine if you show me yours." It's time for humankind to return to its senses, to enjoy the basic pleasures of being alive in healthy bodies without the fig leaf, black dot, or digital squares covering our sex organs. After all, they are responsible for creating the next generation as well as giving us an enormous amount of pleasure.

❧ 13 ❧

CREATIVE PARTNERSEX

Exploring New Sexual Skills

COUPLES THAT AGREE to explore a new range of erotic delights by being experimental are embracing what I call creative partnersex. The first year Grant and I were together, we took a giant leap into creative sex by trying everything we could imagine. Our exploration had us pumping out some major orgasms that soon sparked the realization that I could design my sex life just like I painted a picture. The key was allowing myself to be as creative with sex as I had been with art. It was exhilarating to turn my fear into excitement, and that invariably led to better orgasms every time I had the courage to push through another old inhibition.

For seven years I was married to a man I found sexually appealing and cared for, but our sex life was dismal. The one time I got up the nerve to ask him to slow down when we were fucking so I could come, too, he told me that sex was something natural and couldn't be controlled. I was too uptight to suggest other ways to share orgasms, so we mostly avoided sex. Toward the end of the last year we were married he came home one night and announced he was taking up golf. I blurted out: "That's good, because I'm taking up sex." We both laughed at my remark, but two months later we were divorced and I kept my word.

For seventeen years, Grant was married to a woman he also cared for, but she was sexually conservative. She was concerned about losing her "vaginal orgasms" and refused to let him do any direct clitoral contact during partnersex. She also rejected the idea of verbalizing sexual fantasies, especially since they were things she would never want to experience. Imagine his delight when he did manual stimulation on my clitoris during intercourse while describing a fantasy and I blew the top of my head off with several dynamite orgasms.

After that first experience, I couldn't get enough direct clitoral contact. We looked at pornography together and began sharing our sexual fantasies. Next, I began having orgasms from oralsex after Grant showed me photos of other women's sex organs to prove my genital deformity was imaginary. Out of gratitude, I gave him a blowjob and swallowed for the first time. He coaxed me into letting him trim my pubic hair so he could photograph what he called "my beautiful cunt," a word I had formerly hated. The process of becoming cunt positive led me to paint the first self-portrait of my genitals.

Grant's dining room table was the site of one of our hottest scenes, and me bending over my bathroom sink getting cunt fucked from behind was another winner. We watched ourselves having sex in front of a mirror that was strategically placed by his bed. This led to using a timer while taking photos of us having sex. One of those photos was the inspiration for my first twenty-eight-by-forty-inch full-blown erotic drawing. He also gave me my first electric orgasm with a vibrator. We finally got up the courage to masturbate in front of each other one at a time, which may have been one of our finest erotic moments.

Although Grant and I went on to explore threesomes and group sex, for those couples who want to maintain the boundaries of monogamy, most everything we did during our first year together I would highly recommend to any couple wanting to explore a fuller, better sex life. Other couples choosing to expand their sexuality by meeting like-minded couples to play with sexually will have no problem connecting. Personal ads used to be the source for communicating, but now, with the Internet, all kinds of clubs, retreats, and even cruises are available by clicking a mouse.

After years of having sex with the same person, partnersex can be like eating in the same restaurant where you've tasted everything that comes out of the kitchen. The food is still delicious and nourishing, but there are no surprises. Going to the same restaurant assures you of getting what you want, while a foray to a new one adds adventure and fun. Maintaining culinary pleasure is probably based on achieving a balance between the two. I believe the same principle applies to sex. Similar to tasting a new ethnic food with spices and flavors that are unfamiliar, the first time we do something sexually new, it's scary but exciting. The unknown gets the adrenaline flowing, which can feed into sexual arousal, boosting desire for both partners.

Allowing sexual experimentation into partnersex requires trust, keeping an open mind, and talking freely about how both of you feel after trying something new. Be sure to take plenty of time to discuss what you liked best and what you'd like to change the next time. If one of you dislikes doing something, drop it. There are so many other things to explore. However, I believe a good rule of pleasure is not to condemn something until you've tried it at least once, maybe even twice just to make sure. If it's something your partner is seriously turned on to, maybe going for three would make sense.

Visual images are very powerful. The same as watching yourself masturbating, having partnersex in front of a mirror provides an image of how a couple looks being sexual together. Most people have cameras and many have videocameras. It's fun to create your own erotica. If you are working with still images, put together a scrapbook of your sex life. I made a photo album of my sex life with Grant using an antique book I found in a flea market. The opening portraits were of our genitals in oval frames.

One friend combined commercial porn with photos of her boyfriend and her having sex. Keeping a sex journal or writing down your fantasies is also informative as well as stimulating. If you are paranoid that someone might read your journal, write everything in files requiring a password. For me, drawing sex art has always been a source of arousal. Although I would never have admitted it at the time, drawing and painting the nude when I was sexually repressed secretly turned me on.

The first time I went to the Metropolitan Museum of Art fresh out of Kansas, I nearly swooned when I saw the old masters' paintings of nudes with religious or mythological themes barely disguising the erotic elements. Society's insistence on keeping the subject of sex separate and hidden keeps us from accessing fine-art images of human sexuality. We don't have museums of sex art where folks can go to get inspired, but we do have books with high-class sexual images created by great artists. Nearly every artist has at one time or other done erotic drawings and paintings.

Despite the efforts of the religious right to censor explicit sexual images, porn has become so much a part of American culture that it is being taught at the college level as a legitimate course. My friend Susie Bright actually put together and taught the first course at Santa Cruz, titled "How to Look at a Dirty Picture." Susie once said it's easy to criticize what you don't like about pornography, but it's far more informative to discover what you do like. I totally agree, but as a double Virgo I'm born to criticize.

When I watched my first X-rated video, everything turned me on because sexual images were new. After a few years of seeing live sex at parties and watching women having authentic orgasms with vibrators during workshops, I became bored with the obligatory blowjob to get the man hard, a fast friction fuck with no clit stimulation, and the phony screams of a woman faking orgasm. In the meantime, the men remained focused on breathing and getting what they wanted in order to have their orgasm. My constant criticism of the heterosexual formula in most pornography interfered with my sexual arousal.

Next I went through a period where the genre that turned me on most was gay male porn. Looking at men's muscular bodies going at it equally and coming for real was more interesting than watching a woman being passive while a man fucked her. I have no

LOVERS SHARING MASTURBATION. *A young couple watches a pornographic video they have chosen together while they play with themselves. She has cushioned the head of the electric vibrator with a washcloth over her clitoris in order to vibrate longer before coming. He has the remote control nearby to fast forward.*

objection to men having this kind of porn as a favorite fantasy, but I do have a problem when pornography stands in for sex education. Of course, there are those exceptions when porn is done well enough to actually demonstrate good sexual techniques.

During the eighties, when I was still running my weekend workshops, Saturday night the group would have dinner together. Those who were interested were invited to come back to my apartment to watch some porn. For the most part, these women had never seen hard-core sexual images. First, I'd put on the standard male-oriented porn, and it would have them glued to the screen until the first woman voiced a complaint. Then it set them all off. Next I put on one of the videos produced by my friend Candida Royalle. She acted in porn in her youth and decided to get behind the camera to make her own videos from a woman's point of view. At first the group preferred her softer approach with a love story minus what's called "the money shot," when a man pulls out and ejaculates on a woman's body. But after awhile they lost interest and started talking again. When I put on my favorite gay male porn, it held their attention the longest.

Watching porn and masturbating together can be fun. The problem is finding something that you both like. There is a huge selection of X-rated videos available these days, along with all the soft-core movies on cable. My suggestion is not to watch porn like you would watch a movie—from beginning to end. I fast forward if the story line slows down the action, and when a scene is good, it's worth playing more than once. Sometimes I turn off the sound track and listen to my favorite seventies rock 'n' roll. With a vibrator on my clit, I am less critical of what's happening in any X-rated video.

Sexual fantasy is at the heart of the creative process that requires the freedom to imagine the unimaginable without a censor inside our heads. After years of a sugary diet of romantic fantasies, I worried whenever I found myself thinking about getting tied to a log in the woods by a kidnapper and having a Boy Scout troop find us. The kidnapper, the Scout Master, and the troop then take turns having their way with me. Once I understood that I was playing all the roles in my imagination, it freed me to stop passing judgment on my fantasies.

Now when I fanaticize a rape scene, I know I am both the rapist and the woman getting violated. In a bondage fantasy, I use the idea of being tied down and helpless as a way to imagine sexual surrender or the opposite of being in complete control. Although I have put others into bondage, I have never been tied down and I have no desire to be raped in real life. I use these images to excite my mind and fuel my orgasms.

In developing a more varied fantasy life, I also began probing the recesses of my unconscious mind to uncover childhood memories. Growing up with three brothers and a handsome daddy I adored, I found a wealth of sexual treasures buried in my nuclear family. These memories are labeled "incestuous" and are forbidden. Reclaiming them opened one of the major accesses to my erotic mind.

Sweet memories of sitting in my daddy's lap feeling protected and secure. Playing doctor with my little brothers and the kids down the block. Feeling my older brother's erection under a blanket on the front porch when I was seven. Now I love it when Eric pretends to be my big brother. We are like kids again with the added naughty element of making sure we don't get caught. Even hotter and more forbidden is when I call him daddy while we are having sex, which is actually a more common fantasy for women than society would care to admit.

Women who have never thought about sex will have to start from scratch when it comes to developing a fantasy life. They can begin by discovering and collecting images from reading magazines and books with sexual material gradually building a repertoire of sexual imagery. Watching X-rated videos provides visual imagery. Visiting chat rooms or talking on the phone anonymously is another way to explore your sexual fantasies. One of the best companies for phone sex, Intimate Connections, is posted on my website with detailed instructions if you are new to phone sex.

During the eighties, when casual sex shut down, anonymous phone sex allowed me to revisit my hedonistic days. In spite of all my experiences talking about sex, the first time I began describing myself on the phone, I drifted into being who I actually was and got bogged down in reality. A few fantasy versions of myself were a horny housewife, a famous porn star, or a bisexual nymphomaniac, to name a few. I've used phone sex to get turned on for a session of self-loving after I hung up. When I had a great voice on the other end and we were building a hot scene together, I had the phone in one hand and my vibrator in the other. It was the ideal low-maintenance anonymous sex date where I didn't have to wear makeup or be the famous woman who teaches masturbation.

Fantasy role-playing with your lover or spouse is an adventure into new realms of physical sensations with mental games that create heightened emotional states. This consensual game is based on playing a dominant or submissive role to make sex more varied, fun, and exciting. Couples can explore an erotic exchange of power without the psychological baggage of labels like "sadomasochism," and cliché images of whips and chains. Playing a sex game by deciding who will be in control is simply an extension of what's actually going on in our daily lives without agreements or awareness. Once the roles are spelled out there are more possibilities for new adventures with pleasure.

We know there are many husbands who dominate their wives, or the reverse, wives who dominate their husbands. This exchange of power is unconscious and taken for granted. It's quite different when two adults decide who will be in charge of what takes place in the bedroom and then negotiates a game for sexual pleasure.

Many women have told me they could never take control of sex because they have no idea how to be "dominant." That's when I ask them to recall a time when dinner was nearly ready and one of the kids ran in wanting attention. If she herself is not a mother, then she can easily "hear" her own mother's voice sounding like a five-star general—"Get out of the kitchen this instant! Can't you see I'm busy?"Women wield this kind of power in the home every day, all the time.

Instead of being a silent partner or a drill sergeant in the bedroom, consider the idea of running a sexual encounter with your lover or husband. Some of the roles I have played that have been fun with both women and men are: I'm the teacher and he is my pupil. I'm the mistress and she is my sex slave. I'm the doctor and he is my patient with some genital disorder I must examine and cure. A girlfriend of mine loves to be the whore with a heart of gold who will do anything to please her client. Her husband gives her a hundred-dollar bill that she keeps when they play this game. When the kids were small, they'd get a baby-sitter and he would pick her up in a bar and rent a hotel room for privacy. She said bringing cash into their sex life inspired them both. She really put out and he appreciated her more.

Dressing for sex is a major part of fantasy role-playing. Picking a role and then creating a costume to go with it is as much fun as actually doing the role-playing. Start off gradually. Later, you can buy elaborate costumes if this turns you both on. My first dominant outfit was going topless with tight gray sweatpants, my favorite cowboy boots, and a big leather belt. It was amazing how those few items combined changed my mental attitude. Instead of being a passive, pretty little sex object waiting to be made love to, I became a cowgirl who knew how to ride a bucking bronco.

Your first experience might be having "regular sex" with one difference: You play the usual male role by making a dinner date, choosing a restaurant, making the reservation, ordering for him, selecting the wine, and paying the check while only the two of you know he's wearing a pair of your silk panties underneath his dark blue suit. During dinner, remind him that he must surrender to your sexual wishes later. Most men love this kind of role reversal. He'll find it nice to be taken care of sexually if he's been responsible for initiating sex most of the time. If the opposite is true in your relationship, relinquish your control and promise to be his devoted sex slave for the evening.

Setting the stage is about making your environment inviting with soft lighting, candles, incense, and mood music, and having everything you want to use close at hand. Some basic things to consider are standard sex toys like a battery-operated or electric vibrator, a dildo, and a good massage oil. Or, if you're using condoms, have plenty along with your favorite water-based lube. If there are children at home it's a good idea to have a lock on the bedroom door to ensure privacy.

When you're feeling adventurous, gradually add new items to surprise your lover: a cock ring, a small paddle, a buttplug, and some light restraints that fasten with Velcro. If either of you has any mixed feelings, start off with "pretend bondage" where your partner imagines he can't move. A blindfold alters the experience of sex by eliminating sight; it emphasizes the other senses of touch, smell, and sound.

Later, if either of you wants to be restrained with wrist and leg cuffs or tied up with rope, it's important to read a book that goes into detail about how this is done safely. While some might like the idea of restraints, they can also bring on panic and the person will need to be released immediately. Even a silk scarf can tighten when stress is put on it, so you'd want to have a pair of scissors handy to cut him loose fast. Everyone who does fantasy role-playing with restraints agrees on a word that ends the game immediately. It's like the button on a treadmill marked STOP. If you press it, it will stop. Playing with more intense sensation needs to be learned with a professional in a workshop or by joining a club where scene players meet and share their expertise.

Fantasy Role-Playing requires a more advanced form of sexual communication. Couples can explore each other's fantasies, which will create more intimacy between them. When the game is over, take care of each other by doing a lot of hugging and talking about what you felt and thought while you're still in bed. Most of us have been conditioned to surrender our bodies and souls to love, so consensual SM (slave and master) or BD (bondage and discipline) can become the ultimate romantic scenario.

Couples who want to experiment with threesomes usually start off having it as a fantasy before they actually do it. If the idea turns them both on, then they can consider pursuing the possibility. It's often easier for most women to be sexually intimate with another woman than it is for a man to feel comfortable about inviting another man unless he's bisexual. Each couple will have to discuss this before they proceed. Personally, I needed to establish equal sharing before taking my first step toward a threesome, and Grant agreed. We also thought it was best for me to choose a woman I was interested in being sexual with for the first time. Not the other way around.

FANTASY ROLE PLAYING. *This couple is acting out a consensual fantasy with light bondage; she is the dominant partner and he is her sex slave. She rides him while using her vibrator for clitoral stimulation. His hands are tied to the bedpost with a silk scarf. He watches her enjoying herself while he helplessly awaits his turn.*

The first girlfriend I asked declined, but the next time I made the offer, to another friend, she was very turned on by the idea. We made a three-way date. Grant was sensitive about honoring our primary bond by not going nuts with a new piece of ass and ignoring me. When that happens, it creates a degree of jealousy and dampens the possibility of sharing this kind of pleasure in the future. The night Grant and I had sex with another man was interesting but weird. It was more like the two guys politely taking turns while I got all the sexual attention. They were not at all interested in each other.

There are many variations on three-way sharing. A couple I know enjoys having both women doing oralsex to the man. One husband simply wants to watch his wife get fucked while he masturbates. Other couples enjoy having the women go down on each other followed by him pumping one or both of them. One of my three-way affairs consisted of the husband going down on me while she played with my tits, and then they would fuck each other while I masturbated alongside them. Their agreement was he couldn't put his penis inside another woman's vagina, but she could screw whomever she pleased.

Today, my favorite three-way sharing is taking turns with two pleasuring one and then rotating. It's the same as with a three-way massage, where the people involved decide who goes first, second, and third. During another affair with a married couple, all three of us wanted to go last so we ended up flipping a coin and leaving it up to chance. When we started spending weekends together, sometimes we would pick separate nights so one person could bask in the luxury of getting all the attention from the other two that evening.

Group sex could easily take a whole chapter, but I'm saving all those delectable details for my memoir. There are basically five different sexual combinations; self-sexuality, partnersex, a threesome, and two couples, which is a foursome. It takes five or more people to qualify as group sex. Although group sex slowed down with the advent of AIDS, some married couples never stopped enjoying it. Sex parties made a comeback in San Francisco during the second half of the eighties with the Jack and Jill Off parties that featured heterosexual group masturbation. As people became more comfortable using latex gloves and condoms, the JO parties turned into the Queen of Heaven Parties hosted by Carol Queen and Robert Lawrence. The group dynamic will always have the warmest spot in my heart, since it was my real graduate work in human sexuality.

After all my experimentation with recreational drugs, the only one that enhanced sex for me was marijuana. The fact that marijuana heightens all the senses of pleasure will ensure that the liquor and pharmaceutical lobbyists in Washington will continue to keep it an illegal substance. While some people enjoy a glass of wine before sex because it reduces inhibitions, I find alcohol dulls my senses. None of the psychedelic drugs of the sixties and seventies rocked my boat sexually, and while cocaine and ecstasy were great for dancing, they never improved my partnersex.

Today we have to beware of all the legal prescription drugs. Americans are taking antidepressants as casually as aspirin, and they are known to dampen or totally kill sexual desire. The best aphrodisiac is a healthy body and an open mind.

Designing their own sex lives gives couples an opportunity to go beyond the limitations of each one's personality, the polite and appropriate cover story we show the world. With a little creativity, couples can discover a new sexual persona just waiting to be brought out of the bedroom closet. Go ahead. Take a risk with a little sexual adventuring.

❧ 14 ❧

ROSEBUD

Anal Eroticism for Heterosexuals

I N THE MOVIE *Citizen Kane,* the close-up of Orson Wells's lips saying "Rosebud" was supposedly the last word uttered by William Randolph Hearst. Some claim it was the name of his sled. My fantasy is that rosebud was his mistress's nickname because they were into anal eroticism—a redeeming quality for such a power-driven, greedy man. I can't help but admire those folks who can turn the lowly asshole into a source of sexual desire.

There are common words that are used to refer to the anus, like asshole, poop shoot, bunghole, and bum to name a few, but I have called mine rosebud ever since I've learned to love this powerfully erotic orifice. My other favorite name is buttyhole, because it's the one my mother used when I was a child.

The first time I experienced anal penetration I was twenty-two and madly in love with Tommy. One night after attending a party where we'd had quite a few drinks, we started tearing each other's clothes off the minute we got home—just like they still do it in movies. We didn't make it to the bed but fell to the floor instead. I was on my back trying to wiggle out of a Playtex girdle with my legs in the air when my truly beloved pulled up and nailed me in the wrong hole. When his penis jabbed into my virginal butt, I felt a hot, searing pain. Letting out a howl, I kicked him away, and for the next twenty years no one ever got near my rosebud again.

In the early seventies, on one of my many trips to San Francisco, my friend Arlene Elster was in court defending her right to show porn in the little movie theater she ran on Polk Street. She won her case eventually. One afternoon, while waiting for her, I was standing in the back of the darkened theater watching a scene of a young hippie couple that obviously loved analsex. A close-up of his fat, glistening dick gracefully sliding in and out of her blissfully relaxed rosebud sent a surge of primal desire rushing through my body. From then on, butt fucking was incorporated into my masturbation fantasy repertoire with one variation: the woman was always tied down and helpless.

A year later, my gay friend Bobby and I were talking about sex, per usual. As I listened to him lovingly describe analsex, I admitted I was a little bit interested in trying it some day. Later that afternoon Bobby offered to demonstrate analsex with Billy, my young bisexual lover, while I watched. Billy was a pitcher, not a catcher, and he wouldn't go for it, so I surprised myself by asking Bobby if he would do analsex with me. The healthy seventies were free from AIDS, so all we needed was a bottle of massage oil and our mutual consent. After all, a rosebud is a rosebud is a rosebud.

Bobby worshiped assholes, and for the next ten minutes, he devoured mine with such loving care I was blown away. It was my first experience with analingus. As his mouth and tongue lapped at my tight, defensive little buttyhole, the muscles gradually relaxed. By the time he gently pushed the head of his big oiled dick against rosebud, I was so open and turned on that he eased inside with a minimum of discomfort. Then he slowly fucked me doggie style as I played with my clit. The orgasm was unforgettable. We only did it a couple of more times before Bobby left town, but I'll love him forever.

The following year, during my affair with Laura, we often took turns doing anal penetration with a well-oiled finger while the other one was masturbating with a vibrator. With us it was more health-oriented, although it was also pleasurable. She had a long history of constipation and it was my theory that having an orgasm with anal penetration would help to relax a part of her body that had only been a source of tension. It actually helped me, too. I also began doing anal penetration with some of my self-loving sessions. The best way to approach anal sexual pleasure is to do it with oneself first.

Still, I remained skittish, and very few lovers ever got inside rosebud. It seemed that analsex was a High Holy Day kind of sex that took place only once or twice a year. When it did happen, I always found it to be erotic, but the day after, I had the feeling of an impending bowel movement. There was no pain. It was simply unusual to have this kind of awareness in my anus. Normally, rosebud was totally out of sight and out of mind except when I got constipated. Then she dominated my entire life. Maybe it was raw pleasure anxiety, something I could easily diagnose in others but had difficulty seeing in myself. Meanwhile, analsex remained one of my favorite fantasies for masturbation.

In the beginning of my relationship with Eric, he was so interested in analsex that I was suspicious he might be hiding homosexual tendencies. He told me the desire emerged as a moment of clarity in his typical male adoration of a woman's butt. It was a longing "to experience the sculpted, visceral beauty of the female ass to its fullest." But only if it could be done when the woman took just as much pleasure in the experience as he did.

Another of the many reasons he claimed to like analsex is that he felt most of his girlfriends had responded to it more authentically than vaginal sex. Even when a woman is with an assmaster, the first few moments of anal penetration are a challenge until the muscles fully relax. Seeing one of his college girlfriend's eyes close and jaw drop as she dug her fingers into the carpet was more captivating than when she bucked and screamed passionately during vaginal sex.

As we were talking, I remembered a well-known psychoanalyst once telling me that the most frequently recurring fantasies or repressed desires in his heterosexual male patients was fucking their wives or girlfriends in the ass. He said it came up more often than men wanting to have sex with two women, which I always thought was the number one male sexual fantasy. Maybe this was why so many American men are pathologically homophobic—they are concealing a serious longing for ass fucking.

Naturally, Eric wanted to do some butt loving with me when we first got together. Although I was definitely interested, I explained that during the previous ten years analsex with myself had been with a small buttplug. When I had a woman partner we used either our fingers or the occasional modest strap-on dildo. I wasn't all that sure I could handle his penis inside my usually tight ass. He assured me he'd take great care in going slow. Just talking about analsex was turning me on, but first, I wanted to take an enema to rinse out the lower bowel.

My first enema took place in childhood when my mother used a red bulb syringe to cure a bout of constipation. She was always gentle while applying Vaseline and easing the small black tip inside while saying, "Relax your little buttyhole, Betty Ann." Then, during my fasting and cleansing days in the seventies, I used the standard enema bag and had several series of high colonics. I also have a metal hose with a screw-on cylindrical tip that attaches to the shower, a gay men's anal douching technique—a highly efficient method. Currently I have an expensive, transparent-white, silicone enema bag with a nice long hose and a small case that has several exotic attachments. It is proudly displayed as an objet d'art hanging in my shower.

Although Eric and I have since shared enemas as foreplay to analsex, I prefer taking an enema alone so I can turn the experience into a meditation to mentally prepare myself for this special kind of intimacy. Eventually I learned it was better to clean out my lower bowel a couple of hours before analsex. Otherwise rosebud gets too sensitive from being overstimulated. Besides, right after an enema, some of the water can be retained and come out during analsex. One time a bit of enema water combined with ejaculate came out an hour after we'd had sex while we were sitting in the restaurant having dinner. Waiting helps eliminate these possibilities.

Even better than an enema is when I have a full evacuation with nice firmly packed feces. Simply washing rosebud and inserting my finger is enough preparation then. Residual fecal material just inside the rectum will cause an unpleasant burning sensation for me as well as a thick, dragging sensation on his penis. Now that I have embraced analsex, no one can say, "You don't know from shit!"

That first time Eric and I did analsex and I was clean as a whistle, he began with analingus. In spite of this special treat, I still felt a burning sensation as he began penetration with his well-oiled penis. He kept stopping so I could breathe and relax. At one point, when rosebud finally got over being so nervous and she cooperated, all seven inches glided in smooth as silk. The sensation as always was extremely erotic. He then held still while rosebud got used to having a visitor. With a vibrator on my clit along with his fluid movements and oiled palms smoothing their way over my happy bottom, the orgasm that followed was definitely worth writing home about.

After several months of practice, I began to master the necessary skills that enabled me to enjoy all aspects of quality buttloving. When I am kneeling on the edge of the bed in the knee-chest position with my behind totally exposed, knowing that I am going to get fucked in the ass turns me on. I'm sure this is because anal-sex has been such a prominent feature in my masturbation fantasies, where I imagine being forced to surrender control to endure this forbidden kind of sex—shades of the *Story of O.* It's one of the few instances when I relinquish control and surrender to my partner.

Eric stands behind me slicking up his dick with Charlie Sunshine massage oil. As I'm vibrating my clit, my buttyhole gets warmed up with gentle stroking followed by finger penetration. At this point I'm relaxing the anal muscles. When I feel his dickhead brushing back and forth across rosebud, my desire builds until I reach a level of anal craving. His cock maintains a constant medium pressure against rosebud as I push back into him while tightening and releasing my anal muscles. Breathing and vibrating my clitoris, I rhythmically squeeze the muscle tight, relaxing a moment and then pushing out just a bit. By repeating the process of squeezing, relaxing, and bearing down slightly, my ass literally sucks his dick inside—little by little. After full penetration is achieved, he holds still a moment to give rosebud time to adjust to the sensation of fullness.

This technique for anal entry is great because there is less initial discomfort than with the traditional method, where the other person does all the pushing into a tight, passive orifice. The other important element is that before anal penetration ever begins, the receiving partner needs to be sexually aroused.

I keep the vibes going over my clit as his oiled penis begins to move back and forth at a sweet, languid pace. Indescribably voluptuous feelings spread throughout my entire body. Again, with perfect control, he maintains gentle movement, his inquisitive divining rod probing every inch of my receptive canal. After several minutes I usually request a little more oil to maintain a smooth consistency. As each wave of earthy ecstasy rolls over me, his seamless fucking sends tingling currents up my spine or down my legs. The heat builds until I back up into him, swallowing his hardon with a hungry buttyhole, wanting all I can get.

The sounds I make are often unfamiliar: whimpering baby sounds, the low moans of an experienced whore, or deep bestial growls that come from a primal place within. The wrenching come starts with the orgasm sensation in my clit and spreads into my ass before racing up my spine and out the top of my head into the universe. Just as it has been in the past, the same is true today: First-rate ass fucking always makes me feel extremely vulnerable, and yet, at the same time, oh so powerful.

The first few months we were doing analsex, I dipped in and out of fear. Maybe I was damaging myself or, as the folklore goes, it was unhealthy "going the wrong way on a one-way street." Sometimes my bowel movements seemed fuller and easier, but other times, when I tended toward constipation, I worried that his cock was pushing the shit up into my colon. After all, I'd often heard the expression "fudge packers."

Talking with my gay friend Robert helped to calm many of my unnecessary fears. He assured me that most were based upon myths created by a homophobic society filled with men who feared anal eroticism. I kept forgetting about those reccurring repressed desires in my doctor friend's male patients who longed to fuck their wives in the ass.

Rereading *Anal Pleasure and Health* also eased some of my fears. Jack Morin has the distinction of writing the first comprehensive book on this subject. At one point Jack says it is a good idea to get a sense of how the anus reflects our own lives. Emotions of anger, fear, frustration, or hurt can be expressed by tension held in all our poor little buttyholes. Fear seems to be my specialty. He was right on target when he said we would all benefit from having an imaginary conversation with our mothers to reclaim our anuses from traditional and often cruel toilet training, clumsily administered enemas, or negative messages we received as children from our parents and siblings and later from society.

Although my potty training was gentle and the few enemas I got were sweet, I clearly remember how dedicated Mother was to seeing to it that I didn't bear down to empty my bowels. She was convinced it would cause hemorrhoids later on. She wanted me to relax, rub my tummy, and let my body do the job naturally. This childhood training was so entrenched it took me some time to learn how to bear down slightly in order to facilitate anal penetration.

The first step in beginning to explore your anus is to actually look at it. Many people go through life without a visual image of their sweet little rosebuds. Just as with our genitals, women only look when something is hurting or we think there's a problem. In order to see your anus, you will need a mirror and a good light. There are several positions—standing and bending over, sitting, or kneeling. Be creative and get a good look. I believe this exercise is as important for a woman as examining her vulva. Both men and women need to explore this important opening so they can stop believing the anus is an undesirable part of their bodies.

We all have hair surrounding the folds of our pink or beige puckered buttyholes. Many keep the area shaved—some for appearances, others for cleanliness. I do it for both reasons. There is nothing basically dirty about the anus. While feces have bacteria, most of the organisms are harmless. Excessive fear about anal germs is the result of all the negative messages we get from a society that basically loathes and fears the human body, especially waste products like feces and urine. A recently evacuated bowel with a carefully washed rosebud has fewer bacteria than the average mouth. However, whenever you engage in analingus outside of a fluid-bonded relationship, use saran wrap for protection.

As fixated as we are on personal hygiene and purity, most Americans are walking around with shitty behinds because we rely on a dry wipe after defecation. This is a joke. Once I became sex positive back in the seventies, I used a wet washcloth to wipe my buttyhole after taking a dump or I rinsed off squatting in the bathtub. Now I keep a box of wet wipes on the back of the toilet, which makes it easy to clean up. Every time I wet wipe rosebud these days, I send a few loving thoughts along with some gratitude for all the pleasant bowel movements and hot orgasms she has given me.

If you are new to anal penetration, it's a good idea to begin with your own finger. By tensing and releasing the pelvic floor muscle, it's easy to feel how much movement is present. Along with the perineal muscle supporting the space between the anus and the genitals, there is the pubococcygeal, or PC, muscle that is attached to the front of the pubic bone and circling the anus. Breathing is as important as tightening and releasing the PC muscle, so taking deep breaths all the way down to your anus, and then letting go as you exhale, will help relax the two rings of sphincter muscles that circle the opening of your bottom.

Using plenty of massage oil, gently stroke the entire area surrounding your little puckered friend pressing around at the opening until you feel the muscles letting go. If you have long fingernails, it's a good idea to file them down or at least cover them with a latex glove. Gently push your finger through the folds using the finger pad, not the tip. At the same time, slightly bear down to open the sphincter rings. Before you enter this unexplored place, make sure to add stimulation to your clitoris or penis to commingle positive feelings of sexual arousal with anal penetration. Go slow. Be sweet and gentle. Before attempting anal intercourse with a penis, both partners need to get to the place where they enjoy anal penetration during masturbation.

Remember, one of the basic principles when using a toy for anal penetration is to make sure it has some kind of flared base so it won't get lost inside your body. Anal dildos or buttplugs come in a wide variety of sizes, so start small and gradually increase the size when your buttyhole loves the feeling.

Betty's Blue Hitachment is ideal for those new to anal eroti-

cism. This silky smooth vinyl cap fits over the head of the Magic
Wand vibrator and has a graceful, curved four-inch dildo. Keeping
the Wand on the low setting, the vibrations are a great help in relaxing anal muscles. Once your cute little rosebud surrenders, the
vibrating dildo will be invited inside and the fun begins!
Combining anal penetration with masturbation enhances orgasm
for both women and men.

Two of the most important things to remember while doing
anal penetration is to keep everything well oiled and to go slow.
Forcing the muscles open before relaxation occurs will produce a
burning sensation. Once full penetration is achieved, stop a few
moments to feel the new sensations radiating throughout your
lower body. Men can lie on their backs and use the tip of the
Hitachment to press up into the top wall of the lower bowel. It
might take a little experimentation to find the right place, but
eventually a new sensation will emerge with vibrations and pressure on the prostate gland. This, combined with manual stimulation
of the penis, can result in a totally unique and powerful orgasm.

Those of you who are having trouble with hemorrhoids may
discover that anal eroticism can become part of your self-healing
process. The inflammations are caused in part by chronically tense
sphincter muscles. After having a few orgasms with anal penetration, many of us can stop being such bad-tempered tight-asses.
Women must remember not to go from the anus to the vagina with
the same dildo to avoid getting a urinary tract infection from
incompatible bacteria.

During the past few years, I've experienced some of the most
erotic analsex of my life with Eric. When I began to get a series of
urinary tract infections or UTIs, I was sure it was pure pleasure
anxiety. The entire time I was menstruating, I never had a UTI from
any kind of partnersex. But now that I was postmenopausal, perhaps I didn't have enough naturally occurring friendly bacteria to
maintain an acidic vaginal and urethral environment to ward off
foreign invaders like E. coli and staph bacteria.

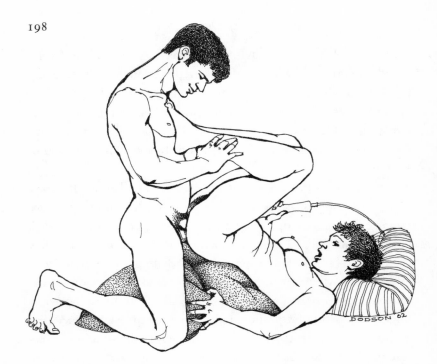

ANAL SEX. *This woman is enjoying anal penetration on her back while using her vibrator on her clitoris. Her feet are resting on his chest with her hips supported by pillows. Any position with the woman on her back is the safest for anal intercourse. Gravity keeps the anal lubrication running away from her vagina or urinary tract, avoiding the possibility of a UTI.*

At one time or other, many women get a UTI, which causes a burning sensation during urination and the feeling that you need to pee frequently. When it's from first-time partnersex it's called "honeymoon cystitis." Although my urologist said there were many factors that cause a UTI, such as bacteria from the skin, I thought mine were the result of my recent analsex. Since I like having analsex on the edge of the bed in the knee-chest position, whatever lube we are using will sometimes seep down, bringing traces of incompatible bacteria into my urinary tract or vagina.

For patients who are prone to UTIs, most urologists recommend taking an antibiotic before and after vaginal or anal intercourse, but I find this unacceptable. Antibiotics destroy the ecology of the vagina and can result in a yeast overgrowth that creates more problems. However, there were several times I ended up taking an antibiotic while exploring alternative healing methods.

I began urinating right after analsex. I drank more water and tried the age-old natural remedy of drinking cranberry juice concentrate. I began eating yogurt and taking lactobacilli capsules and adding a teaspoon of powdered lactobacillus to warm water and douching occasionally. Any pH imbalance is known to be a major contributor to lowering resistance to infections and lactobacilli are the beneficial bacteria that increase the acidic environment in the urinary and genital tract.

While all of these natural remedies helped, for me the only *totally safe* solution so far is having analsex on my back. In this position, gravity pulls the anal lube away from the urethral and vaginal opening. Since analsex is one of our favorites, we are now looking into different kinds of sex slings or swings that attach to the ceiling. That way Eric can stand while I am comfortably lying on my back, facilitating effective analsex for both of us.

In the meantime, we came up with a safe alternative to analsex we call "Double Pen," which is short for double penetration. While I kneel on the edge of the bed with my butt up in the air, I use the electric vibrator on my clit while he slowly inserts a pink-fleshlike, realistic dildo with a flared base into rosebud. The dildo is close to the size of Eric's penis and feels very similar. Since the dildo remains in place instead of moving in and out, the lubrication doesn't get pushed out and seep down into my urinary tract.

Standing behind me, Eric slowly enters my vagina. The sensation of having both my anus and vagina filled extends my boundaries to the utmost—a place that focuses me completely on pure physical sensation. As he begins to move back and forth with his usual care, the anal dildo moves just enough to feel good as his body presses into its base. With the washcloth-covered Magic Wand humming softly over or near my clit, the ascent to high arousal is breathtakingly fast and I can stay there for some time. The orgasm that follows consumes my entire being. He enjoys riding the energy and feeling my muscles contract powerfully when I blast off with a big O.

Over the years I've always enjoyed seeing photos of double penetration in magazines and watching videos that feature it. However, there's a big difference between what's done on screen as opposed to real life. Many seasoned porn stars refuse to do double penetration with two guys, and the ones who do charge extra for it. Penetration by two cocks without adequate knowledge and considerate partners can result in pain as well as be damaging.

This advanced kind of fucking requires an experienced woman who knows how to control the action. She also needs to understand her body, know how to use her pelvic floor muscles and to enjoy intense physical sensations. The two men also need to know what they're doing. Anyone who has seen double pen in porn will tell you the men neither know nor care about anything resembling finesse. So if you do have the desire to take it all, make sure your male partners can be trusted.

For the man who wants to do analsex with a woman, I suggest he master anal penetration on himself first so he knows what it feels like. Then he's ready to propose some buttloving with his girlfriend or wife. Unfortunately, too many straight men think that any enjoyment of anal penetration makes them gay. Believe me, anal stimulation will heighten any "real man's" orgasm during masturbation.

Mark is a heterosexual friend in his early sixties who developed a love affair with his anus. Throughout his sex life, he always enjoyed a woman's finger in his ass while receiving oralsex, but it never dawned on him to do it to himself while masturbating. When he included anal penetration with a small buttplug, he soon discovered that his orgasms were becoming more intense. He's now using such a large buttplug that he can easily understand how gay men can take big cocks and dildos up their butts. Consistently good anal loving creates a hungry buttyhole with the same appetite as a voracious cunt.

After I fully embraced analsex, every so often I found myself regretting all the years I'd been in so much conflict over it, denying myself all those pleasures. When that happens, I stop myself. Instead of dwelling on feeling sad, I remind myself to be grateful I finally got around to it. The same as I tell others to do, I give myself a lecture about staying in the moment, enjoying what I have right now.

Eric and I take turns doing anal penetration for each other during partner-assisted masturbation sessions. We also share analingus on special occasions. He loves it when I massage his entire pup rump, including his peter and balls, while making passes back and forth over his buttyhole. When he's ready, I slowly penetrate him with either Betty's Barbell or the pink dildo, moving it back and forth. He also enjoys pressure on his prostate gland with two of my fingers while he jacks off. With my other hand I can press my knuckles into his perineum or massage his testicles. The concept of a woman taking charge of penetration is as erotic to him as the sensations themselves. We both enjoy doing anal penetration to ourselves when we have our private sessions of self-loving. Anal eroticism is alive and well at our house.

Providing the idea of past lives is true, one of my recent fantasies is that when Eric turns sixty-nine, my age when we met, I'll come back as a hunky blonde California surfer. My dick will be every bit as handsome and functional as Eric's, which keeps on going like the Energizer bunny. When we meet at a party, I will seduce him and become his first male lover. Then I'll move in with him and we'll take turns rump-pumping each other day and night with abandon. You'll have to excuse me now while I go masturbate with my favorite orange buttplug.

❧ 15 ❧

SEXUAL SENIORS

The Beat Goes On

FROM THE CRADLE to the grave, sex is part of our lives whether we love, hate, or deny it. We are seldom taught that partnersex is age-related and that we will go through different phases, but how we practice sex over the span of a lifetime will differ greatly. Most commercial images of sex revolve around people in their twenties and thirties, so many young adults believe the sex they are currently having will last "forever" while older couples reminisce about how good sex used to be. A few seniors feel partnersex grows better with age. Others begin to enjoy leisurely sessions of sex with themselves to their hearts content.

While we might have some sexually active seventy- and eighty-year-old men, there are fewer examples of older women who continue to enjoy sex with themselves or with a partner. This is due in part to the sexual repression women receive and their lack of orgasm. When Oprah Winfrey asked the question on her website whether women were enjoying their sex lives, more than 80 percent said they were dissatisfied. Women can let go of partnersex because it's rarely about pleasure in the first place.

The decade of our fifties begins quite differently for women and men. Many older, successful men divorce and remarry young, attractive women who are called "trophy wives." Some men in their fifties and sixties start second families. Others are having extramarital affairs or keeping a mistress on the side. A few men remain monogamous and sexually active with their wives. However, far more husbands rely on masturbation than society cares to acknowledge. One study showed that over 60 percent of menopausal women in the United States lose interest in sex.

Each of us is unique, so there is no best way to deal with the physical, mental, and emotional changes brought about by menopause. Most doctors will automatically prescribe synthetic HRT, hormone replacement therapy. However, there are alternatives, such as hormones made from the soybean plant. Some women find relief from menopausal symptoms with dietary changes, exercise, herbal remedies, massage therapy, and acupuncture. When it comes to handling this major life transition, each woman must find her own way.

When I went through menopause at fifty, I actually enjoyed my hot flashes and didn't suffer any extreme discomforts. After reading the dire warnings that came with synthetic estrogen replacement, I didn't trust the pharmaceutical companies to have my body's best interests at heart. I decided to make this transition naturally. Growing old seemed to be way off in the distant future. I was feeling vital and happy running my masturbation workshops, exploring fantasy role-playing with women and enjoying friends. My creative project was going through old diaries writing a sexual memoir and taking orgasm breaks when a hot memory turned me on.

The most common complaint from heterosexual women not

taking HRT is painful intercourse due to a thinning of the vaginal lining. Midway through my fifties, I became aware of vaginal discomfort during any kind of penetration with a partner or myself. I knew it was due to a drop in my hormone levels. Being penetrated by a penis, a finger, or a dildo was phased out because it produced pain instead of pleasure, but I continued to enjoy partnersex with women friends while we used our electric vibrators for clitoral stimulation and, of course, sex with myself. As long as I didn't need or want vaginal penetration, I was having a wonderful orgasmic sex life.

The phase of our sixties can present some serious breakdowns in physical health that signals the end of partnersex for some. A lucky few sail right on through in good health. For me, turning sixty meant it was time to re-create myself. After reading *Passages* by Gail Sheehy, I had become aware of the importance of making major changes at the beginning of each decade. After giving it much thought, I decided that my sixties would be devoted to creating videotapes that documented my direct style of teaching. I wanted to leave some kind of legacy for future sex educators.

After nearly ten years of being sexual with women almost exclusively, I began to miss the testosterone-driven energy of men. The idea of entering the straight world in my sixties was very challenging. Lesbians and bisexual women rarely judge one another by our looks or age, so dating within the women's community didn't have the same pressure I felt in the heterosexual world. My advantage was having a reputation, through my books and public appearances, as a woman who liked sex. This gave me dating opportunities the average woman doesn't have.

Still, it took dedication and a fine sense of humor to become heterosexually active, especially as a woman who was not interested in fucking. My first straight affair was having Andy as a JO buddy. I was sixty-one and he was sixty-seven and also single. He lived in a spacious loft above the restaurant he owned. After reading my book, he'd asked a mutual friend to introduce us. When we first met, we discovered we had friends in common from the good old group sex days. Right off he said my book made him feel better about having so much sex with himself.

Andy described his self-loving sessions as something for all his senses—porn for the visual, chocolate for taste, incense to smell, jazz for sound, hands for touching, and a buttplug for anal penetration. I laughed and said he was my kind of guy. When I proposed we masturbate together, he enthusiastically agreed.

We spent many an evening together lying side by side happily doing ourselves while watching porn on a TV that sat at the foot of his king-size bed. Some nights we'd give each other a hand and share some hot talk. This kind of lighthearted sex allowed both of us to have fun on our own terms. We thoroughly enjoyed our low-maintenance relationship, which lasted a few years.

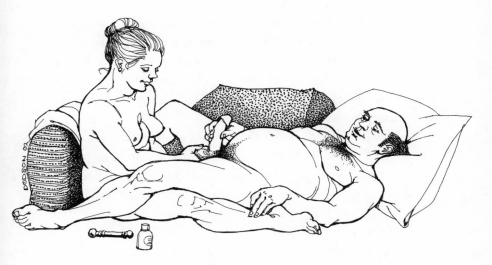

TAKING TURNS. *Partner-assisted masturbation works well for many seniors who need more direct genital stimulation for sexual arousal. Aging bodies can be comfortably supported with an assortment of pillows. Also the use of electric vibrators for both older women and men has become quite commonplace.*

In 1990, I also got a fan letter from a man who'd seen me on television. Heinz was in his late sixties, but looked much younger. He was a great dresser with elegant manners and considerable wealth. He was quite unique in that he preferred women who were over fifty because he found them more interesting. One of his favorite forms of sex was a threesome, which had also been one of mine. After we had enjoyed a couple of three-way romps, it turned out he was into verbalizing fantasies that didn't turn me on and my fantasies didn't work for him. Although we were fantasy incompatible, we stayed friends.

Throughout the decade of the nineties, I spent many weekends with Heinz, his current girlfriend that summer, and his girl Friday, Ellen. My private room and bath overlooked a beautiful swimming pool and bay. As the resident sexologist, I had a lot of fun socializing with his friends, who were my contemporaries. Since I usually hung out with younger people, it was encouraging to see so many straight and gay couples in their sixties and seventies still enjoying life and sex, especially his older gay men friends, who always had much younger lovers. Heinz was convinced that partnersex had never been better than in his seventies. He enjoyed being king and I loved the role of the court jester who defied his golden rule—he who makes the gold makes the rule.

Not long after I finished the videotape of my workshop, I begin fazing them out because of painful hip joints. This began a period of trying different alternative healing methods so I could remain physically active. My sixty-fifth birthday was spent in "enema camp" eating raw food at a health resort in San Diego.

From there I went to finish my second videotape with Samantha, my editor. She had heard about an endocrinologist in Santa Barbara on the cutting edge of the latest in natural hormones. Since Samantha was going through a difficult time with menopause, we made an appointment. The young woman doctor assured us that hormones made from the soybean plant were identical to the molecules formed in the human body. There was no need to worry about the disclaimer that came with synthetic hormones and the long list of warnings about breast and uterine cancer.

At sixty-five I decided to start hormone replacement and revitalize my vagina. When I returned to the East Coast, I found a doctor in my neighborhood. While I told her of my preference for plant-based hormones she listened with interest. Although she routinely put women on synthetic hormones because they had been used successfully for so long, she was willing to work with my request. The plant-based hormones are only available through a gynecologist and a compounding pharmacy. The Women's International Pharmacy in Wisconsin at 800-279-5143 will send you a list of doctors in your area who have prescribed natural hormones. Or get your present gynecologist to work with you.

Within a month of taking all three hormones—estrogen, progesterone, and testosterone—my vaginal lining plumped up and I actually felt horny. Vaginal penetration with a dildo spiced up my masturbation and I began to fantasize a young man's firm cock moving sweetly inside my vagina while I vibrated my clit. After nearly a ten-year hiatus from heterosexual fucking, I had my first penis/vagina sex, and although it was fun, the pain in my hip joints was now making it difficult to open my legs for partnersex. Just when my vagina was back, my hip joints were on their way out.

Two years later I was having a problem even walking. I was immersed in the relentless aging process that showed no mercy as my body turned against me. My world became smaller with each passing day until at sixty-seven I was desperate enough to get bilateral hip-replacement surgery. Within a year, I was a bionic woman with two stainless-steel hip joints and a fresh supply of hormones ready to explore some hot partnersex with men again, until I ran into the next roadblock—body image.

Each new affair required an enormous amount of energy to push through my resistance based on every woman's self-image problem that intensifies with aging. I'd gained weight and the surgical scars made me look like the bride of Frankenstein. There was another deterrent to pursuing heterosexuality. The quality of sex I was having with contemporary men wasn't all that rewarding. One man in his late forties was a good sex partner, but he had so many problems with an ex-wife and sharing custody with their two children that spending time with him was usually a bit depressing.

Once again I was prepared to live out the remainder of my life teaching sex, enjoying my friends, savoring a wealth of sexual memories, and refining my fantasies to keep my self-loving hot and orgasmic.

All of this changed at the age of sixty-nine when Eric entered my life. After our first weekend together, filled with marathon sex that had me in a very good mood, I found myself laughing at the statement made by so many men about angry feminists: "All those women need is a good fuck." Yes, but where are we to find men with the sexual skills to deliver one, especially as we grow older? It's very doubtful I'd be having the quality of sex I'm having now with a man who is my contemporary.

Today I encourage older women not to buy into society's negative messages about sex fading as we grow older. More and more of us need to push aside all of those self-image problems with the monster of vanity whispering, "You're too fat, too wrinkled, or too old to be having sex with a vital young man." As long as older women are willing to initiate sex and they don't operate with romantic expectations of everlasting love, it's a great experience to be sharing our wisdom with a young, energetic man or woman. Many other independent thinkers have followed in the footsteps of the great Greek philosophers Socrates, Plato, and Aristotle, who prized the love that existed between older and younger men. Oscar Wilde, Picasso, and Georgia O'Keeffe all had young lovers, wives, or assistants.

By the time most Americans reach seventy, our agist society expects us to write our wills and get ready to die. This is in spite of recent statistics that show that many seniors live in relatively good health well into their eighties. It's not surprising to find that less stress and more time improves the sex lives of those who remain sexually active. However, many women in this age group outlive the men they married, and they can't imagine finding another partner. While masturbation is a valid sexual outlet, many older women have long since abandoned self-pleasuring—only a handful continue to enjoy their orgasms to the end.

When I turned seventy I realized I was in the youth of old age. It looks as if the rest of my seventies, however, will be spiced up, since I've given myself permission to continue to enjoy sex with my young man. Although I'm fully aware that I am far from average when it comes to sex, I'm convinced one of the important reasons I'm a sexually active senior is because I had a history of masturbation and orgasmic partnersex.

Along with our pleasurable and playful sex and affection, it's been wonderful having Eric to help me out around the house. Since he moved in, I've had the apartment painted, laid new carpeting, installed shelves, and updated my office equipment and furniture. He often works a few feet away from me at his computer stark naked when the room is warm. Seeing his beautiful, strong body and a vase of fresh-cut flowers keeps me in touch with nature as I live happily in the middle of New York City. Although there have been times I've missed my solitude, our camaraderie, with all the playfulness and laughter, is a constant source of joy.

For people inclined to make the comparison between *Harold and Maude* and my relationship with Eric, I can assure them we are quite different. Although I loved the movie, we have been our own sexual lab rats combining his youth and virility with my sexual knowledge and experience, we test out different angles for penetration, experiment with subtle shifts in our bodies, and try new positions.

While companionship and mentoring is highly desirable, there is no stronger glue than sexual compatibility and like-mindedness.

While I have no idea how long our intergenerational affair will last, I intend to enjoy every orgasm and all the affection for as long as it does.

The first year we were together I was pumping out orgasms like an automatic weapon. At the beginning of the third year, there were days my pussy felt like an old musket that could still misfire even with the latest in hormone technology. Although I thought about trying Viagra, the idea of getting a negative side effect wasn't worth it, and I wasn't about to fall for all the hype about Viacreme or other magic potions to enhance female sexuality.

More effective was adjusting my expectations about having the big O every time we had partnersex and adding some new fantasy material. Eric was worried he was not pleasuring me adequately, so I assured him I adored every minute of our sexual connection with or without an orgasm. Although I can still be wiped out by the power of a big come, it just doesn't happen every time we have sex.

When I was in my forties, I remember a friend who was in his late sixties telling me that he had partnersex or masturbated nearly every day, but he only had an orgasm once a week. At the time I remember feeling a bit sorry for him, but now that I'm a sexual senior, I completely understand. Interesting how the first part of my sex life was struggling to have an orgasm during partnersex, and now the second part is claiming the freedom not to have one with every sexual encounter.

One weekend I had an incredible orgasm running a new version of my "Fuck Bar" fantasy. A dozen women are bent over an aperture that locks us in place, similar to the old puritan stocks. The bar's circular counter is above us. Our behinds are exposed, making each woman's pussy accessible. The men walk up to the bar, unzip their pants, and fuck us while they have a drink, light up a smoke, and shoot the shit. My buildup increases as I imagine each man's technique. The revised version has analsex, and if we have an orgasm while on duty we will be punished. But when one client shows up (Eric), no matter how hard I try to fight off an impending climax, I can't help myself and I come.

Several days later I was running the same fantasy while we were fucking, but after making several passes without reaching orgasm, I stopped trying. As I began savoring our connection, I drifted into a kind of erotic meditative state where I floated in my bodily sensations. Most orgasms are over after a few marvelous moments, but this lasted for five or maybe ten minutes as my body shivered and quaked. All forms of sexual pleasure seem to last much longer than they actually do. In the past, after having a big orgasm, if I continued clitoral stimulation with my vibrator I had what I called a "state of ecstasy" as the orgasm energy continued to move throughout my body. This time it was happening without my having an orgasm beforehand—something new.

Since I was not involved in my ascent to a climax, I was more aware of feeling him. He slowed down by sinking his dick deep inside. As we both held still, I felt his cockhead swell as the semen surged into it and then subsided without ejaculating as he relaxed his pelvic floor muscle. When he finally moved toward his climax, I rode his energy until I heard his moan slowly crescendo into a bellow, and I pumped my vaginal muscle on his cock, draining him completely.

We stretched out in each other's arms to wallow in the hormone of bonding—oxytocin. I had none of the feelings of physical discomfort due to pelvic congestion that I'd experienced in the past. One of the reasons women get so grumpy after having sex and not coming is that it can take up to ten hours before the blood drains from our sex organs.

After thinking about it, I figured being in a high state of sexual arousal for an *extended period* of time and then dropping back into *total relaxation* allowed the blood to drain more quickly. The other component was that my deep breathing during our sex session had oxygenated my blood, helping it to flow more freely.

There is no doubt in my mind that fantasy and masturbation grow more important as we age. After having three strokes, my old friend Grant is still enjoying his porn magazines and X-rated videos, happily masturbating as he races toward eighty. When he was ready to go home from the hospital after his first big stroke, the doctor said he might have retrograde ejaculations and the semen would eventually be urinated out. Although he was told to wait a couple of weeks before having sex, his first night home he had to beat off to see if he could ejaculate. He discovered he could still shoot a load, and that was reason enough to carry on.

Today, Grant gets regular massages that include his penis from his young, attractive housekeeper, who is also a trained nurse. When she first started working for him, she spoke only Spanish. Grant started teaching her English in spite of his speech impediment from the strokes. He also showed Maria how to use the vibrator, and she had her first orgasm at thirty-three. They are very fond of one another.

Thanks to my website, I hear from sexual seniors all over the world who are enjoying their sexuality. This is from a man who is sixty-one and a heart attack survivor:

> Without a physical relationship with my late wife I found it almost impossible to obtain sexual relief for many years. Then I met my recent lover and everything worked fine. But the last few times she visited me, I had difficulty with erections. I thought it was my anxiety over failing to satisfy her, but after seeing a clinical psychologist, the term "penile dysfunction" was used. I went to the urology department of the university hospital. Unable to use Viagra because of my nitro-lingual spray, I was given a prescription for Cavaject and it worked perfectly. Within half an hour my lover and I were tearing our clothes off in the bedroom. You've no idea how good it was.

This e-mail is from a postmenopausal woman:

During marriage, I masturbated with a vibrator, having orgasms several times during the day. Of course, hubby was not around to satisfy my needs, nor was his desire for sex as strong as mine. At forty-eight, I had a hysterectomy and things changed. It took a long time to recover any sexual feelings. I felt numb for so long. Sexual encounters with hubby have been few and far between since the surgery, so I continued to take care of myself. Two years ago I went on-line and started going to chat rooms. My first Cybersex was somewhat scary but very exciting, and I begin to recover those feelings that I'd lost after surgery. I was not sure if what I was doing was morally right or wrong.

Now, at fifty-eight, I think a lot of people do Cybersex, and I don't believe it's wrong. It is quite stimulating. I equate it with reading a good juicy novel except now I'm verbally participating in the scenes. I don't seek out lots of different partners and I am very choosy as to the ones I pick. To chat with someone who cares about your satisfaction as much as you care about his can be very rewarding. After all, I believe sex begins in the mind, and what you say you are doing to the other person is very important. Even the idea that the person might be a woman pretending to be a man is quite exciting, too.

Here's an e-mail from a man heading toward ninety:

As an electronic engineer I am constantly impressed by the intricate mechanism devised and installed by nature in the human male, primarily for procreation but happily available for pleasure. Recalling as best I could and factoring the frequency at various ages, I calculated that at eighty-eight years of age, my joy machine has cycled to climax 24,497 times since childhood. My penis has served me well these many years, although it has begun to show its age. I no longer ejaculate. My uncircumcised cock no longer stands at attention to salute its target. It has shrunk about three inches in length but the circumference is the same. On the plus side, the urgency to jack off continues three or four times a week, and believe me, the spasms of climax are as intense as ever. I cannot help but wonder where I would stand on the scale of my peers. None of the surveys I have seen include men over the age of seventy-five.

Since I have joined the ranks of sexually active seniors, goddess willing, I hope to document what happens to older folks past seventy-five who remain sexually alive and well. While I'm not crazy about the aging process, I am thankful for inheriting good genes and having good health. I'm looking forward to enjoying the rest of my seventies and designing the decade of my eighties with yet another sexstyle that I promise will not be age-appropriate.

I'll be forever grateful that I emptied my living room of all the period furniture and turned it into a space where I could run workshops and hold feminist gatherings. Since 1970, this modest twenty-by-twenty-two-foot room has improved the lives of countless women who had the courage to join me in the pursuit of sexual pleasure. Today, when people enter the room, most comment on how beautiful it looks even though it's simply furnished. I'm convinced people are responding to all the orgasm energy that has been stored within the room. Teaching women how to have orgasms turned out to be a fabulous career. From monogamous wife to erotic artist, sexual adventurer, and sex educator, I'd do it all over again in a heartbeat.

❦ 16 ❧

SEX COACHING

Teaching Sex in the New Millennium

S CIENTISTS AND EDUCATORS HAVE BEEN investigating
the complexities of female sexuality for many hundreds of
years. However, the one glaring omission has been the rel-
evance of self-sexuality in healing women's sexual problems. The
remedy to this omission is providing women with the means to
gain sexual self-knowledge. To address this problem, I have been
teaching basic sexual skills that will enable women to have orgasm
through self-stimulation. Once a woman takes sexual pleasure into
her own hands and claims her genitals as her own, she can explore
her body and mind to discover her sexual desires. Then she can
share this information with her partners.

An adult woman who has never experienced an orgasm often
feels less than whole. Everywhere she turns, she is confronted with
idealized images of romantic lovers having passionate sex. She buys

sex books and devours magazine articles on "How to Please Your Man." Yet she rarely receives any useful sex information that deals directly with "How to Please Yourself." Without any experience of self-pleasuring, her sexual ignorance and neediness sets her up as a potential victim, a target for an unscrupulous, sex-starved man who is more than ready to take advantage of her. He's not necessarily evil, just responding to primeval urges of the instinctual brain.

In contrast to a victim, every sexually sophisticated woman I've ever known is well aware that men fake love to get sex just as women fake orgasm to be loved. Her healthy ego and self-esteem allow her to master some form of birth control. She is more likely to avoid situations that might lead to date rape. A total person in her own right, she doesn't desperately need a man to have a sex life or to pay her way.

Sexual and financial self-sufficiency gives a woman a choice of lifestyles. She might want to devote her life to a career. If she chooses to marry, she has a better chance of making a more thoughtful decision. It is my strong belief that an orgasmic wife and mother has greatly increased odds for having a happy married life with well-adjusted children. Experiencing sexual pleasure on a regular basis improves everyone's quality of life. That is why I have stayed the course, teaching women about self-induced orgasm since the early seventies.

Today I work directly with individual women using a system that grew out of twenty-five years of hands-on teaching in my workshops. I call it Sex Coaching. Although I have often said I teach people how to have orgasms, I'm actually teaching a range of masturbation skills so each woman can discover her own orgasmic process and develop her individual style and preference for experiencing sexual pleasure. I also provide information that will improve partnersex, such as demonstrating positions that facilitate clitoral stimulation during intercourse along with the best way to incorporate sex toys.

My clients are basically middle- or upper-class women who are successful in their own right or have married moderately well. Many are divorced. Some are lesbians. They represent a cross section of ethnic groups. These women are educated and therefore a more sexually motivated group. They come from all walks of life and represent every profession. The age range is from early twenties through fifties. I've also worked with seniors in their sixties and seventies. The oldest woman who had her first orgasm was eighty-three.

A Sex Coaching session begins with a thirty-minute conversation that includes sharing some good laughter or shedding a few tears as a client talks about her sex history. To model speaking honestly and frankly, I share some of my own experiences, both positive and negative.

When I ask a client about her current experience with orgasm, many simply don't know if they are having one. More than half turn out to be having small orgasms, but they are unable to identify them because they are expecting a climax to be like a cataclysmic seizure. Others think high arousal is an orgasm. A few have what appears to be a full-body orgasm, but they're convinced nothing happened. Most of these women have no memory of childhood masturbation and they have lost interest in trying to masturbate as adults because they feel nothing and get discouraged.

A woman who comes to see me knows in advance that she will actually be masturbating while I coach her. Even if she has read my book or watched my video *Celebrating Orgasm,* which documents five women's private sessions, I still go over the process in detail, making sure there are no surprises. I explain I'm like a dance instructor teaching basic techniques. Or a spotter in the gym who will encourage her to push through her current limits of tolerating pleasurable sensations in her body.

She is then asked to disrobe and I offer her a T-shirt to wear, explaining we will be working with massage oil. Another consideration is that any amount of nervousness lowers the body's temperature and I want to make sure she feels warm. A few women prefer to be completely nude, which is fine. I remain clothed.

The first process allows each woman to claim her sex organ as her own, which is central to her being able to enjoy sexual pleasure. As we sit on the floor together to begin her genital examination, I often discover she has never looked at her genitals in a freestanding mirror, which frees both hands to explore her self inside and out under a good light. Some have taken a cursory look to see if something was wrong under poor lighting with one hand tugging at an outer lip. This gives a distorted view of the vulva. Maybe that's why so many women believe their genitals are unattractive. Imagine what we'd think of our mouths if we only saw them with one lip pulled over to the side?

Adjusting the makeup mirror so we can both view her sex organ together, I aim the bright light between her legs and immediately make a positive comment pointing out a detail of her particular style that's pretty. Many women are shocked and remain silent, while others make a negative comment. A rare few admire what they see.

After she covers the palms of her hands with oil, she is asked to massage the entire genital area with long, gentle strokes. The degree of tentativeness I have observed when a woman first touches her own sex organ is shocking; it's as if she is feeling something so foreign it might harm her. We stay with genital massage until she feels some degree of comfort.

As she is guided through the intricate folds of her vulva, I make analogies to shapes in nature like a flower or a shell or architectural styles like Renaissance for the elaborate drapery of long inner lips, or the simplicity of Art Deco. We locate the shaft of the clitoris and she pulls back the hood to expose the glans. We discuss what she wants to call her sex organ as I suggest clitoris, pussy, vulva, cunt, twat, or a more personal nickname. The most common name for our sex organs is vagina. It's safe because it limits female sexuality to the birth canal and procreation. Including the clitoris questions how men have been doing intercourse for centuries. Some women choose pussy or vulva while others want to think it over. I tell them that since my mother named me Betty Ann, I call my sex organ Clitty Ann.

We then go on to discuss concerns over dangling and uneven inner lips, moles, skin tags, coloration, and texture of the inner and outer labia, search for lost and found clitorises, observe vaginal secretions, discuss genital hygiene, and put to rest a few imaginary genital deformities.

Many women today know the importance of doing Kegel exercises. For those who don't, I explain that PC is short for pubococcygeal muscle, which is sometimes referred to as the pelvic floor or vaginal muscle. When I tell a client to lift and squeeze the muscle, at first many tighten the surrounding muscles in their stomachs, thighs, and buttocks. For best results she will want to eventually iso-

GENITAL EXAMINATION

late just the PC muscle. A toned muscle ensures better orgasms, overall genital health, and bladder control, and helps to regulate bowels. Doing PC exercises can shorten delivery time and restore vaginal muscles after giving birth.

Looking into the mirror, as she lifts up to tighten the muscle, she can see her entire genital area move, including the clitoris. Then she inserts a finger inside her vagina to actually feel the muscle contract. I tell her that's what her partner will feel on his finger or penis. When she withdraws her finger, I encourage her to observe the amount and quality of secretion and to smell her scent, explaining it will vary with her diet, menstrual cycle, and genital hygiene.

Most clients think any kind of vaginal discharge indicates an infection or that something is wrong. I calm their fears, saying we all have mucus inside our vaginas and the quality and quantity of it changes according to where we are in our menstrual cycle.

For those women who are not having partnersex, or doing any form of penetration, it is especially important to aerate the vagina by inserting a finger or using Betty's Barbell. I also recommend she insert her finger inside her vagina before having partnersex to check her scent and flavor. This will allow her to feel more secure about receiving oralsex. It's a body check similar to testing our breath or taking a quick sniff of an armpit for reassurance that we're okay.

Some badly neglected pussies can smell pretty raunchy. Just imagine how our mouths would look and smell if we never opened them or brushed our teeth. In a few cases, it wouldn't have surprised me to see a few moths flying out of a neglected vulva. I've seen bits of toilet paper caught in pubic hair, old dried mucus, or a thick vaginal discharge from lack of use and care. I've helped clients eliminate bad cases of dried smegma under the clitoral hood with a Q-tip and oil. With one client, we extracted an old tampon that had been there for two weeks.

We discuss trimming, shaping, and shaving the pubic hair. It not only facilitates cleanliness, but pussy grooming gives a woman a good opportunity to get to know her sex organ better. Some women come to me already waxed or shaved, but that doesn't mean they have a good relationship with their genitals. Some shave in the shower by feel and never look at themselves closely, or they have a professional bikini wax done not to please themselves but because their boyfriend requested they get one.

Finally, I bring out the diagrams of the entire clitoris that are published in the book *A New View of a Woman's Body*. She gets to see the internal anatomy of the clitoris and the parts that become erect during sexual arousal: the clitoral glans, legs, bulbs, and urethral sponge. Helping a woman understand her genital anatomy as well as seeing her vulva as a source of beauty, pleasure, and power lays the foundation on which she can build an orgasmic sex life.

I'm happy to say that well over half of my clients end up appreciating the form and function of their magnificent sex organ—the divine vulva. The rest need a little more time to process the experience, but chances are good they will get there eventually. I often hear from women six months, or even several years later, saying they have finally come to appreciate their vulvas.

Next, we move over to the center of the room and she lies down on her back on a soft blanket with several pillows. I sit alongside her close enough to put my hands on her body. Her legs are bent, knees up with her feet flat on the floor. She is asked to take a few deep breaths and make sure she's in a comfortable position. Some women appear uncomfortable, so I suggest adjustments of the pillows or a shift in her position. I remind her of the importance of being comfortable whenever she is having sex with herself or another person. Then, with one hand at her hips and the other on the side of her arm, I gently rock her so she can let go of tension. The laying on of hands is reassuring and nonsexual.

Learning to successfully masturbate to orgasm as an adult woman can happen quickly or take time. I discuss the elements she will be using to build sexual desire that will eventually lead to orgasm: breathing, pelvic thrusting, vaginal penetration, and using the PC muscle. During the session, she will experiment with three different kinds of clitoral stimulation—fingers, a battery-operated vibrator, and an electric vibrator. It's perfectly okay if she doesn't have an orgasm during the session. Our work together will still be successful because now she will know how to practice when she gets home.

Breathing is first and foremost. While she is masturbating, I want her to hear herself breathing out loud. Her jaw needs to be relaxed, which allows her mouth to be slightly open. Modeling, I take air in through my nose and exhale through my mouth. After a few moments of breathing together, I ask her to make a sound as she exhales. Again I demonstrate making a sound similar to a deep sigh. Many of us have been so severely conditioned to remain silent during sex that some can't even sigh out loud. Later on she can practice saying "yes" or "more" or any word she chooses during her own self-loving sessions. This helps signal her body that something is feeling good, and later it will be a way to let her partner know when he or she is doing something that is turning her on.

Next is pelvic movement. She starts off with a gentle rocking of the hips that can be perpetual motion for most of her masturbation. She is asked to move her hips in a circle, to free up the pelvic hinge, and then to stretch up as far as she can and bounce her hips up and down. Then I tell her to move her pelvis like Elvis or do the fuck motion that we've all been told is unladylike. Right before having an orgasm, her body will naturally go into a more urgent thrusting action. When she is at home, I recommend she listen to her favorite music and see her masturbation as a sexual dance using the moves that feel best. Eventually she can watch herself masturbate standing in front of a mirror.

After applying massage oil, she places the larger ball of Betty's Barbell just at the vaginal opening. First she focuses on relaxing her vaginal muscles, and then I ask her to squeeze her PC muscle several times on the ball. Another deep breath to relax the vaginal muscle, and the Barbell is inserted one inch. Going slow, she continues to squeeze and release the muscle until the Barbell gradually sinks in all the way. Once inserted, the one pound weight of the Barbell holds it in place leaving both hands free.

Many women have chronic vaginal tension from experiencing pain instead of pleasure with clumsy penetration by an uninformed lover. Although they might be well-meaning, because of their own anxiety or lack of information, they dive into a virgin vagina way too fast without any additional lubrication. Several women who have been diagnosed with vaginismus (chronic muscle contraction) eventually got the small end of the Barbell inside their vaginas by working the PC muscle and using their breathing to relax the muscle.

With the Barbell in place, she begins to rhythmically squeeze and release the PC muscle while rocking the pelvis and coordinating her breathing. As she rocks forward exhaling, she squeezes the PC tight. Then, inhaling, she drops back and relaxes the muscle. Or, if the reverse feels better, she can inhale rocking forward and exhale dropping back. The PC muscle can be held for several breaths and also be left alone to rest.

At first it sounds very complicated, but I explain that it's similar to learning a new dance step: In the beginning we feel awkward and self-conscious, but after some repetitions the body takes over and the moves become automatic. There is no one "right" way to use any of these techniques. The important thing is to breathe, rock, and squeeze the PC muscle until her individual style emerges.

Once penetration feels good and she's comfortable working her PC muscle against the Barbell, I have her add clitoral stimulation using several manual techniques that I demonstrated during the genital exam. Always using massage oil to keep everything gliding smoothly, she tries two fingers on either side of the clitoral shaft moving up and down, a finger on either side of the clitoris, or several fingers circling the entire clitoral area. As soon as she says nothing much is happening with her hand, I give her a small battery-operated vibrator called The Water Dancer to use on and around her clitoris. After five to ten minutes I ask how it's feeling. If she still isn't getting much sensation, we move on to the electric Magic Wand.

Most clients get good feelings with all three kinds of stimulation, but at some point, they eventually drift. When a client is happy with her hand or a battery-operated vibrator, she can stay with it. However, during a session, I suggest she experiences all three types of clitoral stimulation just to know what's available. With the vaginal Barbell in place, she uses one hand for her choice of clitoral stimulation. Her free hand can stay in touch with her body and enhance desire by pulling up on the pubic mound, pressing into the bladder area, doing breast massage, nipple teasing, or reaching down and moving the Barbell in and out.

With the electric vibrator, she starts off with her clitoris under a washcloth folded into four layers. As she vibrates, I encourage her to breathe while coordinating her pelvic movements and pumping the pelvic floor muscle. She is reminded not to rely on pressure only with the vibrator to increase arousal. Keeping the massager in motion while using a light touch is a simple technique, but it must be learned. Gradually she can reduce the washcloth layers to increase the sensation on her clitoris until she ends up with one layer. The reason I recommend staying with at least one layer of washcloth is to allow each woman to last longer before coming.

The most common misuse of electric vibrators is coming within moments by using it directly on the clitoris without any form of cushioning. The other problem is using pressure only to increase sensation, which actually does the opposite—it numbs the clitoris and will eventually cause an unpleasant burning sensation.

Right after her first orgasm, instead of stopping, she's shown how to lighten up by doubling the washcloth again or putting her hand over her clitoris. She is encouraged to continue vibrating, moving, and breathing. Within a few moments, hypersensitivity of the clitoris passes and she can keep going to experience some lively contractions and aftershocks of pleasure. It's a shame to miss this extension of sexual pleasure. With conscious PC muscle pumping, pelvic rocking, and breathing, she can simply enjoy riding these waves of sexual energy or move into another sexual buildup and go on to have a second or third orgasm.

For women who have no idea what they like or what feels good when it comes to vaginal penetration, or for those who ask about G-spot stimulation, I offer to demonstrate different techniques. By now most clients are completely relaxed and we have established a mutual trust. While she continues using the vibrator, I sit between her legs. The Barbell is still inside. Very slowly I pull the Barbell out, and as I do so, I tell her to tighten her PC muscle. When she relaxes the muscle, the weight of the Barbell allows it to sink back in. After repeating this several times, she is asked to try it for herself.

Next I angle the Barbell up toward the vaginal ceiling and press into her urethral sponge, G-spot, or prostate gland, whichever name she prefers. Some don't like it. Most, like myself, think it feels pleasant and a handful say it feels great. In order for her to angle the Barbell, it's easier if she is sitting in a semireclining position. Then I demonstrate what I call a "slow fuck," moving the Barbell in and out while she controls her own clitoral stimulation. This is contrasted with a fast friction in and out movement. Of all three types of penetration, the majority of women say they get the most sexual sensations with a slow in and out while they work the PC muscle on the Barbell.

A consistent pattern I see in the women coming to see me is that they don't spend enough time doing self-stimulation. During a coaching session a client usually goes for an hour or more. Some go for nearly two hours building sexual desire. They are amazed when they finally get to deepen the experience of sexual pleasure before and after orgasm with a tireless electric vibrator and a sex coach who encourages them to continue. Using a vibrator with skill makes getting there and enjoying the autonomic chills and thrills after the first orgasm as good if not better than the actual climax itself. The ability to have serial orgasms is available to most women if they simply don't stop and just continue vibrating. Many clients have two or more orgasms. Most are grateful but a few are angry that it took so long to discover this capacity for pleasure that was there all along just waiting to be tapped.

Wilhelm Reich's concept of "pleasure anxiety" has been very useful in explaining why so many clients end clitoral stimulation the minute it starts to get really good. Feeling anxious because waves of thrilling sensations are racing through our bodies sounds ridiculous, but I have consistently observed women stopping at the moment they are about to free-fall into sexual ecstasy. Having me there to assure her she's okay allows her to go farther than when she's on her own.

Some women worry about damaging their body by coming more than once. Others think they might have a heart attack! They need constant reassurance that it's okay. Once they have a second orgasm, I often tease them about becoming "sex pigs." Laughter helps. Since we are all coming from sexual repression, it takes some time and reassurance to accept these new experiences of sexual intensity.

Observing women's bodies over the years, one of the first signs of building sexual arousal or tension is when breathing becomes deeper. As the level of sexual excitement grows with a more rapid heartbeat, the woman often breathes like someone who's been jogging around the park. There is increased muscle tension. Pelvic movements become more urgent. Some women's legs tremble. A flush on her face and neck sometimes appears. A few break a sweat. Her mouth is open. Her eyes are usually closed and she is concentrating intensely. She can appear to be in pain with extreme pleasure as her face goes into contortions. She is usually gasping, crying out, groaning, or making sounds of pleasure at the moment of orgasm. A few remain silent.

Behaviors that indicate a woman might be faking pleasure are when her body is totally relaxed without any movement, or just the opposite, when she is thrashing about as if she's out of control.

Being overly self-conscious or constantly looking to me for approval means she is not focused on her own sexual sensations. Talking the whole time, laughing inappropriately, or holding her mouth, jaw, or body rigid represents fear of losing control. Screaming is an unconscious display of frustration and anger rather than passion.

When I'm working with a screamer, I remind her she needs to be taking in oxygen with deep breathing, not making sounds similar to a bad sound track from an X-rated video. In saying that, it doesn't mean I'm against making loud sounds. But those high-pitched screams tighten the vocal cords and lock the energy in the throat. Instead, I encourage her to deepen the sound by taking it down into her belly and allowing it to come out more naturally on the exhale.

Orgasm need not be excessively dramatic, but the body will have some kind of autonomic contractions. The upper body usually lifts and the pelvis tilts up as though to meet it, making a U curve. The opposite, an arched back, often indicates a woman is pulling away from pleasure. Reich described this as the "hysterical arch" (see page 65). Sometimes the pelvis or whole torso will snap with aftershocks of pleasure following a big orgasm, but there are always exceptions. One girlfriend of mine remained silent and her body barely moved when she climaxed. Her face appeared peaceful and calm. There were minimal external signs of sexual excitement except the muscles in the front of her torso tightened. Her sexual process was internal with strong pelvic floor muscle contractions, and unless I had my finger inside her vagina, it would have been difficult or nearly impossible to know when she had an orgasm.

The current approach to sexual dysfunction developed by The American Psychiatric Association (APA) divides sexual problems into four categories of disorders: desire, arousal, orgasm, and pain. These disturbances are assumed to be universal physiological sexual response patterns for both women and men. In 1999, a group of twelve women who are all clinicians and social scientists created a feminist critique of the current sex problem nomenclature, offered an alternative vision, and began an activist campaign. They criticized the shortcomings of the APA framework for leaving out women's complaints of emotional, physical, relational, and cultural conflicts. They also correctly fear that if the current marketing patterns with men are indicative, the pharmaceutical industry will aggressively advertise drugs for women's sexual dissatisfactions with a one-size-fits-all approach. *A New View of Women's Sexual Problems,* edited by Leonore Tiefer and Ellyn Kaschak, is available from Hayworth Press.

While I agree with the complexities of dealing with female sexuality, and I'm aware that a poor woman in any devastated country doesn't have the luxury to pursue any aspect of sexual pleasure, here in America there are many women who do. I'm all for experimenting with aphrodisiacs, hormones, and even pharmaceutical drugs to increase a woman's sexual desire and arousal potential. However, let's not lose sight of the fact that the magic pill just might turn out to be women's understanding of how their sexual bodies function once they explore their own genitals with self-stimulation. For many non-orgasmic women, plugging in an electric vibrator and using it correctly can bring the most neglected of clitorises back to life. Remember, the Magic Wand is to women what Viagra is to men.

Whether a woman chooses to avoid sex with a partner or to enjoy sharing orgasms on her own terms, the acceptance of masturbation is central. This would be a modest beginning to end American women's sexual dysfunction and to create a theory of female sexual pleasure that honors the multi-dimensionality of our lives. As I said in the early seventies, socially institutionalized, dependent partnersex is depersonalizing. Masturbation can return sexual pleasure to its proper place—the individual.

Because I believe the future of sex education will include sex coaching through the practice of masturbation, I've established The

Betty Dodson Foundation, a nonprofit organization. The vision of the foundation is to further the sex education/information that I have created and/or accumulated for women and to extend it to include men and couples. The foundation will preserve and build upon my art, writings, books, videos, and sex information gathered on the website. Along with training Sex Coaches, videos that detail this innovative method would be made available to sex educators and therapists worldwide. Direct coaching/teaching by a person trained in the sexual arts would allow adults to master sexual skills that can be practiced, refined, and shared, creating more harmony in partnersex. Physical affection is one of the greatest sources of human contentment.

America spends trillions of dollars on technology making the latest in military planes, tanks, and guns. Trillions more are spent on traveling to the moon and back and sending satellites into orbits that circle Earth, establishing instant communication systems. Yet we have little or no technology about how to enjoy our relationships and our sexual bodies and how to raise happy, well-rounded children. As science leaps forward it seems that our quality of life loses more ground. Since I believe that thought creates form, I hold the image that in the near future we will have a science and technology devoted to the heavenly pursuit of sexual happiness so we can enjoy our earthly garden of delights in healthy bodies and minds.

Afterword

My website was launched in 1996 with my old friend, onetime lover, and writing mentor, Grant Taylor, as the Webmaster. When he first brought up the idea, I was only mildly interested in the Internet. Technology was moving way too fast for me to keep up. For the life of me I couldn't understand the concept of a World Wide Web—an electronic cloud of data surrounding Earth that anyone could access with a computer and telephone wires. Grant reminded me that I didn't fully understand how electricity worked either, but that never kept me from flipping the switch on my vibrator. He made his point so I eventually agreed. After working on my mission statement, Grant and I gave birth to www.bettydodson.com, which has turned out to be our best collaboration yet.

The website quickly grew and soon millions of visitors were dropping in each month. At the end of the first year, I began to realize that the Internet was my first completely uncensored form of communication. Editors of newspapers and magazines consistently censored my views about the importance of masturbation. A few network television talk shows interviewed me when *Sex for One* came out. But I was better known by European television viewers than here at home. Amsterdam had me on their big Sunday night talk show and showed a portion of the video about my workshop. In contrast, even bold HBO showed only the women's faces during the brief segment on my masturbation workshop for the series entitled *Real Sex.*

For Grant, learning HTML language and building my website served two purposes: first, it was his therapy for developing new parts of his brain after a stroke took away his ability to speak and write; second, he was fulfilling his boyhood dream of publishing a sex magazine. More than once he'd ended up in the principal's office after getting caught drawing popular cartoon characters involved in sexual acts or showing off their sex organs. The Genital Art Forum is one of his favorites. People send us photos of their cocks and cunts (I prefer the old Anglo-Saxon terms) along with an essay about the relationship they are having with their sex organs. The Genital Art Forum remains a sexual healing for society's fig-leaf mentality. Hiding our sex organs is one of the cornerstones of the foundation of sexual repression. This shame is based upon the idea of original sin that was invented and enforced by organized religions.

Ask Betty is my favorite labor of love. Two days a week I answer questions from my website visitors. My responses are not based on the formulaic approach of traditional therapists who adhere to the coital imperative of women having orgasms through "vigorous penile thrusting inside a vagina after adequate foreplay." Instead, I advocate some form of direct clitoral stimulation all the way through orgasm just the same as men have enjoyed from the beginning of time. I guess by now you have picked up on this concept since I've been yammering about it for the last two hundred pages.

One of the biggest concerns for men and women visiting my website is whether some feeling, idea, or sexual activity is normal.

People desperately want to be "normal"—the universal ideal of social acceptability. Instead, I'm all for sexual diversity and creativity. As long as any particular sexual activity is between one or more consenting adults and no one is harmed, I say get the sex you want. Of course, that statement assumes a person understands enough about sexuality to know what he or she wants. Finally, I am a huge fan of self-sexuality. I'm convinced that masturbation is the major source for many of our orgasms, with partnersex thrown in occasionally. Whether or not our partnersex is mutually orgasmic depends on both people involved.

Now with my website, I continue my commitment to introducing sexual pleasure into the feminist dialogue. My ideal of sexual freedom follows a similar path as that of my suffragette hero, Victoria Woodhull. In 1873, the then "scandalous" Victoria stated: "I never had sexual intercourse with any man whom I am ashamed to stand side by side before the world with the act. I am not ashamed of any act of my life. . . . And if I want sexual intercourse with one hundred men I shall have it. . . . And this sexual intercourse business may as well as be discussed now, and discussed until you are so familiar with your sexual organs that a reference to them will no longer make the blush mount to your face any more than a reference to any other part of your body." Today the public discourse by most feminist leaders, scholars, and educators is primarily centered on some form of abuse, disease, or dysfunction. We can openly talk about women's sexual pain and suffering, but goddess forbid we openly talk about how we have our best orgasms. One thing is clear to me: As long as we continue to insist that the only "right" way to be sexual is within a monogamous heterosexual relationship, men and women in a position of leadership will continue to avoid discussing the subject of pleasure for fear of being outed. The fact that they are not having any sexual pleasure would be as embarrassing as having too much or the "wrong" kind.

I look forward to the day when going public about who we are as sexual beings will be no different than discussing our favorite foods, movies, sports, or hobbies. Through my website as well as many others, there is now a sex-positive movement with millions of activists joining together on the barricades against sexual ignorance. If you're a friend of sex who would like to take a stand for pleasure, start today by enjoying your own selfloving sessions without any guilt or apology. Telling a few friends about your favorite masturbation or partnersex techniques with a description of one of your better orgasms qualifies you as a budding sexual activist in my book. Come join me in cyberspace at bettydodson.com for the erotic renaissance of the new millennium and we'll celebrate sexual pleasure together.

ABOUT THE AUTHOR

Betty Dodson went public with her love of sex in 1968 when she had the first one-woman exhibition of erotic art in New York City. Whether she is drawing, painting, writing, teaching, or producing videos, sexuality has been the subject off her life's work.

By the early seventies, teaching women masturbation skills and an appreciation of the aesthetics of their sex organs became her feminist commitment. She also began writing articles to express her ideas about women's sexual liberation. In 1973 Dodson left a successful art career to begin teaching and writing about sex full-time. Over the next twenty-five years the women in her workshops shared the truth about their sex lives and explored the varied experiences of orgasm by sharing group masturbation. Her first book, *Liberating Masturbation,* was self-published in 1974 and became a feminist classic. *Sex for One: The Joy of Selfloving,* published in 1987 and revised in 1996, became a bestseller.

Dodson received a Ph.D. in sexology from the Institute for the Advanced Study of Human Sexuality in 1992. She has a private practice in New York City and maintains a website: www.bettydodson.com.

A WORD FROM BETTY
ABOUT HER ILLUSTRATIONS

Without giving it much thought, I agreed to provide illustrations for the book, a decision I would temporarily regret. Even though it had been nearly two decades since I'd drawn anything except for an occasional sketch or two, I assumed drawing was like riding a bicycle—you never forget how. But after drawing every day for nearly a month, I was convinced I'd lost all my skills. One day, in desperation, I started repeating out loud what Bernard Klonis, my drawing instructor at the Art Students League, used to constantly say, "Draw through the form." Finally, the first illustration came off the end of my Rapidograph pen and I was elated. Drawing turned out to be a joy, as I spent some time on the other side of my brain. I could draw and talk on the phone, listen to music, or think about everything or nothing. Working in pen and ink was wonderful and demanding.

The diagrams of genital anatomy were taken from several sources. First, I want to acknowledge the work done by the Federation of Feminist Women's Health Centers. The illustrations by Susan Gage in their book, *A New View of a Woman's Body,* were a major resource. I also used information from the *Color Atlas of Anatomy* by Johannes W. Rohen and Elke Lutjen-

Drecoll, medical doctors at the University of Erlangen in Germany. And finally, the art of Frank H. Netter, M.D., of the CIBA collection of illustrations, was my first introduction to detailed drawings of the human reproductive organs.

One of the most interesting discoveries I made was that every artist has his or her own version of how to represent the anatomy of the human body. The images varied greatly. My personal inter-pretations may not always be entirely accurate. Still, they will give my readers some idea of the marvelous design of the human body, especially our magnificent sex organs.